||||||| ||||||||||||||||||||| |||
I0135016

ACCELERATED LEARNING

Proven Scientific Techniques to Learn Absolutely
Anything

(A Comprehensive Guide for Beginners to
Improve Your Skills)

Margaret Collins

Published by Bella Froast

Margaret Collins

All Rights Reserved

Accelerated Learning: Proven Scientific Techniques to Learn Absolutely Anything (A Comprehensive Guide for Beginners to Improve Your Skills)

ISBN 978-1-77485-336-8

All rights reserved. No part of this guide may be reproduced in any form without permission in writing from the publisher except in the case of brief quotations embodied in critical articles or reviews.

Legal & Disclaimer

The information contained in this book is not designed to replace or take the place of any form of medicine or professional medical advice. The information in this book has been provided for educational and entertainment purposes only.

The information contained in this book has been compiled from sources deemed reliable, and it is accurate to the best of the Author's knowledge; however, the Author cannot guarantee its accuracy and validity and cannot be held liable for any errors or omissions. Changes are periodically made to this book. You must consult your doctor or get professional medical advice before using any of the suggested remedies, techniques, or information in this book.

Upon using the information contained in this book, you agree to hold harmless the Author from and against any damages, costs, and expenses, including any legal fees potentially resulting from the application of any of the information provided by this guide. This disclaimer applies to any damages or injury caused by the use and application, whether directly or indirectly, of any advice or information presented, whether for breach of contract, tort, negligence, personal injury, criminal intent, or under any other cause of action.

You agree to accept all risks of using the information presented inside this book. You need to consult a professional medical practitioner in order to ensure you are both able and healthy enough to participate in this program.

Table of Contents

Introduction

This book outlines the most effective steps and strategies on how to learn, retain bits of data, and access the information when you require it.

In the world of life there are three constants: change death, and the emergence of new information.

A lot of students believe that the thought of study seems like an overwhelming task that is a symbiosis of information and endless hours of slaving in front of a laptop or in front of a book, and some cups of coffee.

It's not necessary to need to be this way Well, it's not always that way at all, anyway.

While this approach to studying might be effective for some however, it's not for all. The mistake made by these group is to force them to absorb information in a way which does not help their comprehension.

Learning, after all has shifted gradually from memorizing to applying and analysis.

And who wants to spend their entire time with a block of text? It's a beautiful day. Your Internet has arrived. Your buddies are enjoying themselves. There's more to life than school.

Chapter 1: Define assessable Goals

When you begin to learn something new, you must set up measurable goals that you can achieve. The goals should test your knowledge or skills without obscurity. When you come to your goals it is important to make them interesting and challenging. If you consider reaching these goals in the timeframe you've set and you feel exuberant and excited. Although you must make goals that are difficult for you, be sure that you don't make them too complex that you're not sure you can achieve them. However, you should not make them too simple that they lead you to lose the interest. When you begin to implement the lessons you learned from this book to your personal life, you'll begin to realize that goals you previously thought was unattainable are now within reach and it can be a great feeling. The reason why you should set realistic and interesting objectives for your life is that the brain is naturally wired with an desire to exert effort toward the goals. If you have an end goal that you are aiming for, all your focus and effort will be focused on creating it in both conscious and unconscious ways. The majority of your learning takes place without conscious thought, in your own mind. If you have a goal that you're thinking about, even if you're not contemplating it your brain is thinking about it, adjusting with it and making connections with it, and then building on it.

The more significance your subconscious mind attaches to the new skill or knowledge the more efficient it can help you achieve your goals. The more specific goals you've set more easily it will be for your brain to grasp them and work towards their goals. Make your goals as precise as you can to ensure that your brain has an easy direction to follow. The less clear your goal the more your brain is likely to struggle with it. If you make your goals measurable as well as stimulating and real your mind will get into full force and will do whatever it takes to realize them. Once your mind is set with clearly defined goals, it is able to anticipate and go through every stage of the process, beginning with the final result and then tracing it back to the present. This will help you determine what must be accomplished and learnt to complete every step. It will regularly assess your current position in relation to where you're going, and then use the information to determine the next step is.

If you are thinking about the new skills you have acquired and the direction you'll need to take be sure to think about where you are at. So you'll have an idea of the specific areas you should focus on in the future, based on your experiences from previous mistakes you made and applying what you have learned from these to avoid similar issues later on. Determining an objective that you can measure is always a great way to give your progress an extra boost. Additionally, it's crucial that you define your own objectives and don't let anyone else set the goal for you.

You know your goals more than you can. Before you set your goals it is recommended that you have read about the elements discussed in the mind-set section in this guide. Goals for the short-term can aid you in gaining speed through your process of learning however they should be part of a larger, long-term target. Individuals who belong to the category of entity are scared of goals and the idea that if they fail to achieve their goals, then they're not competent. This attitude can be detrimental and put them in an attitude that they're not capable of achieving their goals. Always try to adhere to the incremental mindset. If the idea of setting goals that you must strive towards is intimidating then you're still exhibiting the traits of an entity-thinker. Work hard to find ways to get rid of this limiting and untrue mindset.

Give Your Goal a boost by imagining it

Our brains are designed to respond to different ideas of our desired outcomes. It is important to establish a clear goal that you can assess. This is particularly effective when you include tangible experiences like sound, touch, taste, and smell. If you can create a visual in your mind of the outcome you want to accomplish it is possible to grasp something that is solid and then move toward it. Start by establishing the outcome you want in your head along with the benefits you can expect from it. This is especially helpful when you are feeling discouraged. Begin with the end objective, and then go back in steps to anticipate what actions you should take next. Continue this process all the way to the current moment. Determine precisely the skills you require to can focus which can help you to save time. Tim Ferriss, for instance had a desire to speedily learn the tango. He had set a target to reach finals in the Buenos Aires tango championships. He visualized the event in his head often and then classified it into different aspects he'd need to focus on in order to reach his target. He studied dancers from earlier championships and realized that those who performed the tango that had broad fluid movements had a higher chance to progress further into the championships. This knowledge led him to focused on learning this particular kind of tango, which saved him time. Let's imagine that you want to master a specific language until you are self-sufficient living in that particular country. It is possible to set intermediate objectives in the meantime for example, like passing an exam in the timeframe of a specific number of months. With this in mind it is possible to conclude that the addition of skills like writing and reading aren't essential if your primary aim is to speak and comprehend. When you've made this decision then you can concentrate your attention on learning techniques which are based mostly on audial and verbal strategies. This will help you achieve your aim through breaking down the goal into distinct areas you can concentrate on.

Imagine your goals even for a short time will assist greatly in making them more realistic within your head. Additionally, you will decide what the most effective ways to get there. Most people do not have clearly defined goals and are unable to visualize these goals. Beware of this mistake. The brain is wired to respond to visual prompts which will speed up your advancement. Set your goals and visualize them in front of you. This can be done with any purpose, for example, studying for an examination. Imagine yourself passing it with excellent marks and decide what steps you must take to reach the desired result beginning from the place you are. Perhaps you could begin by looking up past tests that covered the same subject, and focusing your studies on the particular subjects that were addressed on those tests. This can cut the study requirements of your students drastically and will save you a lot of time. This highly effective technique of working backwards towards the goal you want to achieve will be discussed further in the second chapter of this book.

Determine Potential roadblocks ahead of time

The rough times you will encounter in your journey to learn will happen. In order to prepare yourself for and better over them, you should figure out what obstacles you'll encounter while working toward your goals. The more you visualize your goals before you, the better understanding you'll have of the route you'll need to take. It's not unusual to anticipate possible obstacles before they actually appear. Make a plan and then come up with various strategies to deal with them ahead of time This will allow you to prepare for the most effective way. In the next section you will learn one easy way to give yourself an enormous boost in achieving your goals.

Make Yourself Accountable Add Stakes into"Prize Pool. "Prize Pool"

The "easiest" method to reach your goals in learning is to add penalties for not finishing your work within the timeframe you have set. Yes, there is an "consequence" being not getting additional benefits in the end all. But nine times out 10 that's not going to be enough for everyone.

It may be a bit surprising for certain people however, having that additional stress on your shoulders can encourage a large number of people. If you're taking that path, make sure that your results are truly powerful. It's important to take a toll if you fail to reach your objectives. Whatever life throws before you, the only thing that ought to be on your radar are the negative consequences of not achieving your goals.

You'd be feeling it if you were to lose $100, would you? Consider one of the goals of your process of learning that you give $100 to a family member or even to a stranger. The added sting will inspire you to avoid losing the money you have invested. Sites such as stickk.com are a good place to begin.

In addition, people are social beings , and you can use this for your benefit. If you're trying to master something, you should find an individual who will work with you. This is applicable to any task you're trying to do (for instance losing weight or lose weight). The presence of someone in your life who can be there to critique your actions when you go off the direction you want to go is a fantastic motivational factor.

It is obvious that they must be someone that you consider with respect and would not wish to disappoint. It could be a significant person or a close friend or even a parent person should help you be in the mindset. These risks are only one aspect of the adventure ahead.

We can't simply get ourselves down and hope just that as motivating. There should be some benefits also. In the next part, we will go over the benefits of this.

Early Rewards Early Rewards, Early Motivation

People are inclined to think of the one major reward at the conclusion of an exhausting job to help them feel motivated. It could be a mistake due to the fact that all the time will be unsatisfying. To progress you must have a sense of motivation.

What better way to motivate yourself than a few "quick victories"? They don't have to be a lot of fun. The only thing you should know is that the brain associates your experience with a continuous reward. Make an overwhelming task appear enjoyable by setting small rewards when you take small milestones towards your ultimate success.

Some abilities already come with "built-in" rewards set for you. The ability to play tennis or chess will gradually help you beat your opponents more frequently. The ability to learn a new language lets you to talk with more sophisticated ways as you advance in your classes. Speed reading allows you to read faster and more efficiently. These are motivating factors by their own.

Remind yourself of these little victories. These are the victories that will propel you to your ultimate goal. The thing that many learners do not remember is how to harness the self-motivation abilities in their mind. You can give yourself a applause every when you make a good effort.

Alongside manipulating your brain to make work enjoyable, there's an added benefit to this strategy. If you do make mistakes, they'll not be with the same force! But it is important to be proud of your achievements while you're learning. There's no better way to approach it. Sing or dance, hug someone, give a high-five to your acquaintances, drink an espresso, or go through a few pages of your favourite author.

Beyond these small, incremental reward, make sure you take advantage of a larger one after you have achieved something bigger. An evening out towards the end of the week, a film together with the S.O., a relaxing massage or spa treatment. These are only examples, so you are at ease to tailor your rewards according to how you feel best. Note them down when you've achieved something important, mark the item off the list.

Many people prefer to begin by tackling the difficult aspects of mastering a skill. Consider getting into break dancing before you've mastered how to move your feet in the beat. This is only for individuals who want to jump straight into the tough part of the process.

To stay focused, using this method it is essential to continually remind yourself of the small rewards. They're the primary motive behind why you keep moving ahead, no matter how hard it gets. As an example, suppose you're playing against one who could be considered an expert.

Instead of worrying about the fact that you're not winning games be happy every time you take some of the game pieces. For every time you put them in a "check" position. All it is in your mind at the moment. However, in the near future, you'll enjoy your first "checkmate and be a great feeling.

Some prefer to consider their mistakes as successes. In reality that you need to begin seeing these as wins too. In the end, failure is a normal part of learning and improving your self-esteem. This is vital to becoming more proficient in your learning, but the best method is that which we will discuss below.

Chapter 2: Building good study habits

You probably have figured out that not everyone uses the same method of learning. The development of great learning skills is dependent on the way you learn. The process of developing good study habits but, it isn't the same for everybody.

1. Find out your own learning style.

After you've finished the first chapter, took a few questions, and thought about the previous exam and study issues and made a guess about the style that you believe is best for your needs. You've also tried some tests and concluded that "kinesthetic certainly is the way you study!" (Note: change the kinesthetic style to suit whatever you like).

Think back to which topics were most easy to study to prepare for your academic professional career. It was it European history? Geometry? Basketball? What type of basketball did you choose to pass that test or subject? The method of learning that allowed you to retain more information at a faster rate is your style of learning. It is important to create the right habits to match this kind of learning style, so you can be more efficient and enjoyable experience when you try to master something.

2. Make a study plan.

Quantity over quality. Learning your lesson is better than spending valuable time reading your textbook and then getting a grade at the final. This is why knowing your individual learning style is the most crucial.

Don't bind your self to the chair in order to complete a chapter if you are able to learn the same amount by performing it. Don't take part in study sessions with a group when you're not able to retain any information later on, or at all. Find out what is most effective for you and use it to your advantage. If you are a fan of different methods to learn, make sure that you have enough space to study all subjects. Develop a study plan and adhere to it if it is effective, or modify it if you think it could be improved.

3. Keep your focus.

Even if every single circumstance on earth could have been ideal to study, if you don't feel up to do it, you could end up wasting your time. If you are creating an outline of your study schedule, select certain times of days that you know that there are no other obligations that could cause you to regret the decision to do your research. If you are required to be studying each day for a long duration, perhaps a few tools will be able to help you throughout the process.

* Got a crush? Why not turn your crush into a meme by saying something that can motivate you to complete your task?

* Download productivity applications. In addition to making you focus on your subject they also give you little

animations, or even additional money for other games you're interested in.

* In fact, using any type of reward system could aid in your efforts to keep going. What if you gave yourself a treat each when you've completed two paragraphs of the paper you're working on? You can also enjoy some YouTube content from your favourite channel after every chapter?

* Keep a to-do list. Every item you cross off from your list provides the feeling of satisfaction. It also helps you to be more motivated as you feel that you have accomplished something important in your life.

• Take breaks throughout your studying routine. This can be viewed as a reward. This is a motivator in its own. However, spacing your studies can aid in reviving the brain after the constant stream of information. When your body and mind are refreshed after a good break, you'll be able to maintain a an improved outlook when you are studying the next section of your class.

* Look for locations where you are driven to study and don't have any other other activity other than research. It's best to have several places in case your place of choice is crowded!

Set reasonable guidelines. Strive for perfection can cause problems, particularly when you feel that you're not doing anything even with your efforts.

4. Concentrate.

One of the biggest challenges for students these days is the sheer amount of distractions that surround them. From television to the internet phones, games on mobiles, eating out, calling friends or drinking, and the latest controversy involving Kim Kardashian... there are so many things you'd prefer to do instead of studying!

Focusing and concentrating is among the most essential learning skills to master. There will be times when you won't be in the quiet of a room, and also, you won't always be working on an assignment you enjoy. Find a way to control your focus and keep it focused on the most important things.

Tools that help you concentrate on studying are basically identical to the tools you use to keep you engaged. To-do lists and productivity apps can help you stay focused on the tasks that you must do.

5. Unsure of something? Have a conversation with a friend!

Perhaps your teacher or a close family member or anyone else who's been through with the subject before. Even the most knowledgeable person on earth may not know everything. It's only a human. It's best to get the facts clear the issue when it first occurs since the lessons typically are built upon previous lessons. It's harder to catch up rather than take a problem to the root.

Chapter 3: "Right On" Time

As we've said that everyone has different desires in their lives. Certain people wish to be successful in business or in the field of education, while others prefer to remain at home and be a parent. Many want to fill their time with a variety of interests, and others are looking to make their life more enjoyable through exercises or meditation. Naturally, based on your objectives you'll need to concentrate on various aspects in various ways to accomplish your goals, but there's one rule that all regardless of their goals must follow if they want to have any chance of success.

This aspect (which you might have already suspected based on the Chapter's name) is what keeps all the facts moving forward. It keeps us from being for indefinitely; it's existed since before we were born , and will continue for a long time after we're gone. If you're still not figuring it out, the issue is that it's time.

If you're trying to be disciplined The regular hour and minute hands on your typical clock could be your best friend or most fearsome foe, based on the way you utilize it. If we had unlimited time to handle all the things we needed to accomplish like school, work or relationships, housework exercising and reading and more. It would not be a necessity for self-discipline since we could just get to these activities when we're feeling the mood. We don't have endless time to live and, as a result of the ancient Egyptians that we have just 24 hours within the course of a single day. In reality, it's an unfortunate fact that, even in the modern world, we have only a tiny part of the time that we have.

According to the majority of health experts that the average person requires approximately eight hours of rest each night. So, after getting those z's at the end of the day, 33% of your day has almost gone. Also, the typical 9am-5pm working hours are what the majority of people are working, this leaves most of us with only eight hours to get started on what we would like to do to live our lives.

However, we're not done yet. Let's look at it further. A typical person will spend 40 minutes to one hour each day driving between work and home. In addition you'll spend an additional half-hour to two hours each day focusing on their health, nutrition and if in school - their academic requirements (i.e. making food, going to the restroom, doing homework, washing, brushing teeth). After all that is completed it's not beyond the realm of possibility to believe that a normal human being - when all of their obligations at school or work are finished and personal requirements are met and taken care of - will have approximately three or four hours per day to achieve their goals.

However, let's face it; there are a myriad of ways for people to use the time further in this age in which we're constantly bombarded by gadgets that are specifically designed to consume our precious hours. According to one study an average American spends between an hour and forty minutes navigating their numerous social media accounts each day! Personally, I've had issues with this and while averaging 90 minutes per day may seem like an overstatement but I think it's likely to be within the realm of possibility of burning off that part of your spare time by checking Facebook, Instagram, Twitter and Snapchat several times every day.

The thing is that you have goals, however they might be but in order to reach them, you have to work towards your goals. In order to accomplish this it is necessary to dedicate time. Based on the things you've read the way that the majority of your time is now gone before you even are able to focus on your goals, the question might be what do I do to accomplish this? How can I achieve my goals that require a significant amount of time, time I do not have?

The good news is that, even though we're not able to control the amount of time we get however, we are able to control how we spend the time we have.

In the next four steps, I'll detail the ways you can get the saddle on your own free time, so that you can ride your horse all up to the goal you want to achieve!

1. Scheduling

(actually making an agenda)

The most crucial step to take in controlling your time off is to determine the exact amount of time you have available and break the time accordingly, by writing it down. This may sound simple, but I'm unable to describe the number of people that I know who only have their schedule in their heads and believe that they will be able to finish everything. People tend to forget things and I don't want to break it to those who believe that you can attain the highest productivity by doing this I'm here to tell that, sooner or later, you will forget something that you might have remembered if you wrote it down.

No, you do not need to carry notespads and pencils with you at all times since you already have a smartphone of yours? That one that's close to your right now or maybe the device that you're reading this book on? The thing you're using isn't just a great tool to keep you connected to things and people you require to be in touch with, but it's your personal assistant who can assist in making the most of the time you have available so that you can make progress towards what you'd like to achieve.

All you have just open up a blank notepad or list application (I prefer Evernote) each Sunday night or prior to the day you'd like your week to begin - and name it What You Need to Do This Week. Simply write down the things you'd like to achieve during the week.

Exercise

Begin planning your trip now.

Clean out the house and place items on Craigslist

Etc.

2. Break it down

Once you've got your list, you have to determine how much time you have available and then divide it up to fit your agenda accordingly. It can be helpful to break things down into weeks days but you can decide how you want to do it.

Example:

Exercise Time: for 3 hours (Monday 7 am - 8 am (Monday 7 am-8 am, Tuesday 7am-8 am and Friday 7 am-8 8 am)

Begin planning your trip now Start planning your trip: two hours (Monday 7 pm to 8 am and Thursday (7 9 pm-8 7 pm-8)

De-clutter and sell items online Time: Two hours (Tuesday 7 8 pm-8 pm, Wednesday 8 9 pm-9 at)

This way you will be able to clearly determine when you should begin doing something and the time that you must accomplish it. This can be very helpful in achieving both short- and long-term goals since it helps break the task down into manageable pieces that don't overburden you in one go.

3. Utilize the rollover method

A new way of life can be difficult, especially one that demands more discipline, as you're likely to experience something different from your previous way of life. This is why, when you begin your list of ways you'd like to manage your time, should not try to accomplish excessively fast. Set yourself a few easy tasks to start off with so that you can ease into the habit of how you work. After a couple of weeks and have become confident with the quantity of tasks you've completed it's okay to add additional things in the mix.

However, as an added benefit If you not complete everything within the course of a week, for that, for example, you wrote down all your tasks, but you didn't get to building your bookshelf, you should carry that project over to the next week that you write your list of tasks. This will ensure that what you note down is accomplished at some point. It is also sensible to write down a strict number of items that you have on your weekly list, and to not add another item until you have completed the job from the week prior to. This allows you to not get caught up in the many tasks you didn't get to in previous weeks.

4. It's as simple as doing it

(even just a bit)

It is likely that you've heard that the most difficult step on any journey is the very first one, which is a matter of debate however, one could claim that by making your list, you've completed the first step. However, I do not agree. If you don't actually begin doing the things at the top of your agenda, you've never really begun. Everyone can write things down however, to actually take action on them is a sign of your commitment to them and puts you on the path to becoming an expert in discipline.

Even with all your efforts there are bound to be problems. Guaranteed. You may have experienced a difficult day at work or perhaps you didn't get enough sleep and aren't "there" sufficient to focus at completing the items you have on your agenda. It's possible that you're not going to complete anything, and you put your agenda on hold and sit in front of the television for three hours after you return home.

Though the temptation to make this choice is overwhelming, especially if you've had a bad day, I suggest to stick to your schedule at a minimum. This is a dangerous slope if you miss a day due to one day can turn into two, then two into three and when you realize it you've gone through a month by and the first week of chores is unfinished. It's ok to make changes to your schedule as you progress. If you have to take half an hour off a task that you had thought of spending an hour, it's acceptable. Any improvement regardless of how small or insignificant, is better than no progress at all.

If you're feeling like I'm lacking the motivation to complete things on my list, focusing on what you'd like to accomplish helps. Although they might seem as if they're a duty at first , especially when you're exhausted from a long morning, however remember that you are the person who recorded them at the beginning. Perhaps it was you just some weeks or even one month ago however it was you. So you know that it's certain that you want to take these actions. If you're not doing these things, you're not leaving anyone down except your self.

I've already said it, and I'll repeat it here (and possibly later too) Self-discipline is all about developing and maintaining healthy habits. Whatever your objectives are, to reach them, you must perform the work necessary, and in order to accomplish that work you must be accustomed to doing it. Habits, dear reader are formed through repetition, and it is created by - yes, you've guessed it, the use of a schedule.

It's obvious that we're human beings, and we don't have the power to control time. However it's not about controlling time in itself however, it's about the way we use that time. I can assure that some of the most successful individuals achieved their success not through whittling off their spare time in a haze instead of focusing their energy like a laser beam toward the goal they wanted to accomplish. The way they achieved this was certain to be a schedule adhered to like glue. To add a little incentive I've noticed that by following a consistent schedule, my time were not as fast since I became more aware of time , rather than being unable to notice it when it passed by me. This is also logical as, in the words of legendary Leonardo da Vinci, "Time lasts long enough to those who utilize it."

Once you have an understanding of why you should be avoiding doing any kind of excessive activity and how to limit it, we'll explore how this method of thinking, along with a solid approach to time management will assist you in building your habit of self-control so you can eventually achieve your objectives.

Contrary to what you might think, I do not believe that motivation is necessarily a negative aspect. In its own way, I believe that it can create an inaccurate view of what they must accomplish and what's expected from them when they start the process of a new endeavor. However, when it is used in conjunction with self-discipline, I do not think it's out the realm of possibility to suggest that motivation is beneficial.

As an example, suppose you've just completed an extremely stressful day at work and when you leave your office, you recall that in your agenda you've scheduled an exercise routine. You're tired your only desire to do is to go home and unwind and once you're in your vehicle, you begin heading toward your home instead of going to the gym. Here's where motivation could provide some assistance. If you are able to make yourself up, inspire yourself, you could get that spark that inspires you to change your thinking. Since you're an organized person, you've got your exercise plan ready to go and are likely to be on the path to reach your targets.

In conclusion motivation can be a risk to be detrimental in the event that it serves as a catalyst to initiate something. However, if your already committed, having a bit of motivation to to get going on your planned tasks you know you have to complete might be of assistance.

Chapter 4: Learning

Create a passion for learning. If you do, you'll never stop growing.

--Anthony J. D'Angelo

When people think about their experiences in school they envision the toughest elements of the experience. But , you're wiser! You know the reason why your brain needs to be stimulated prior to beginning to study. You are aware that you need to have a deeper understanding regarding the science of education or the way you can master.

Let's suppose that you're ready and fired up to take on new challenges. What are some ways to improve the manner you think? What are the best ways to ensure that you're an effective learner? After you've gathered an understanding of the brain and how it's a waste energy if you're not mentally ready and excited about beginning, this section provides a number of methods and strategies that can be used.

Maybe, we could consider a reductionist approach to learning, which assumes that it's the sum of a handful of techniques and methods of learning. But this isn't an accurate assumption. Learning is complex and hard to master. The strategies are only one aspect of the overall. If we assume that learning is an iceberg, the technique is viewed from the top. What lies beneath the water--the mental and emotional self-knowledge we've been making an effort to find and the unknown areas that are yet to be found--would constitute the main element that has been which is not visible to the outside.

When you realize that you're deliberately preparing to begin learning and you realize that you're not able to accomplish the things you want to then you will be required to go through a series of stages to be able to qualify in your chosen field of study.

Consider driving a car as an example. At first you don't even think about the fact that you would like to learn how to drive. You realize that you aren't able to do what you'd like to. Perhaps, as a teen, you've watched the driving of one parent, and you began contemplating what that would be like. You may have had an older brother or sister who you believed to have more fun than you due to the fact that they were able to drive. So, you are taught how to drive but you have to go through each step of the procedure with the utmost diligence, paying attention in the mirrorusing your indicators and then setting off on the road in a mechanical manner, moving both ways when you try to reverse the car to the parking space that is small.

In the end, you'll be able to accomplish everything without being conscious of what you're doing. You could shift gears in the car, and then glance in the mirror between times and engage in conversations as you do this.

In other words it is an amazing turnaround from not knowing the fact that you weren't competent as a driver, to becoming highly proficient, and you can drive around without paying any focus on it. The majority of experts believe with this normal order of development:

Unconscientious incompetence turns into conscientious incompetence that then transforms into conscientious competence and then, finally, unconscientious competence.

This process is crucial in learning. Despite the growing demand for this method the systematic exploration and definition of this subject have not been accomplished. These are the main components of the concept of learning: they are pertinent and essential for learning.

The amount of education that is done in solitude opposed to that which is accomplished in an ensemble

The decision to take a course through the internet

The reading of books on learning and using the media

Planning to utilize an approach and ensuring that it is followed

Infusing how others behave or behave

The distinction between informal and formal learning experiences

Journaling your experience

Techniques that repeat or reinforce are not often employed

Determining the extent to which learning is passive or active

Learning from other methods of learning

Separating learning into different segments of "hows"

Continuously expanding your knowledge about methods of learning from all sources

Recognizing that a significant portion of your learning comes from remembering facts or information, rather than watching or by trial and trial and

Making an effort to comprehend techniques or methods to learn until they are less challenging

Explore your learning style regularly

Reminiscing about both pleasurable and uncomfortable feelings that are triggered by different learning experiences

The focus should be on improving the ways you learn.

Exploring various ways of learning

Selecting learning opportunities that will require you to make use of your skills

Utilizing mind maps or web diagrams

Making use of a learned principle such as that of the learning cycle, or the idea of multiple intelligence

Be thinking about your motivations for learning, both the fundamental ones, and those that motivate you to learn.

Utilizing patterns to activate your memory

Utilizing different techniques and styles of study

Understanding the different roles people take on when they study in an entire group

Learning to deal with the emotions and feelings that are a part of the process of

Giving an answer to the question, How can I improve my ability to learn?

Learning techniques that are adapted from others

Getting used to the unexpected, non-intentional things that happen and working out what they could teach you about knowledge

Participating in activities that help you improve your learning abilities and/or get the most value from your weak points

Understanding who You Are as a Student

It's not a surprise that you'd want to know more of who you are. Some of the areas you could study in our study include the following:

Recognizing that a lot of your learning happens in solitude or when you are part of a larger group.

Recognizing the amount of passive learning versus active learning that you are engaged in

Recognizing that a significant portion of your learning process is taking in new information, versus the process of learning from previous experience

The Art of Learning new techniques 5RS

So far in this book, you've been taught a lot of innovative learning strategies and have also been taught this "preparing to study" techniques:

Infusing how others behave or behave

Reminiscing about both pleasurable and unpleasant feelings triggered by different learning experiences

Think deeply about the motivations to learn, the basic ones, and those that motivate you to learn.

Understanding the various roles that students take on when they study with each other

Learning to deal with emotions and feelings that are a part of the process of

Most of the other methods mentioned are necessary to help you be more efficient as a student. Let me take you back in time to when that you were still in school. For most of us, the fundamental skills or tools of our childhood were described as the three Rs: writing, algebra and reading. Although these are essential skills but there are many other abilities to develop in the current age of information.

Guy Claxton, a British academic has published a fascinating study of the discussion in Wise-Up The Problem of Lifelong Learning [11. Guy Claxton proposes a new three-ractor model: reflection resilient, resourcefulness, and reflectiveness.

He says that the forever student should be focused on the new areas of effectiveness.

They are more broad than the prior 3Rs. In reality, they are a reference to the real world where learning can last forever and the skills and behavior are more important than the acquisition of particular knowledge.

I agree with his views but there are two more relevant aspects such as recalling and the ability to respond. The basis of learning is memorization specifically memorization of techniques and methods instead of learning facts. In today's world memory for facts has become becoming less important. It is the capacity to change that is the real characteristic that continues to be required by learners to change the way they conduct their lives.

Don't think of the old 3Rs and instead consider the 5Rs that are more effective which include resourcefulness, recalling, the ability to reflect, be responsive and resiliency. These are the skills that form the foundation for the ongoing efficient learning in learners.

Learning All About Learning

Awakening to the notion that learning is as crucial as numeracy and literacy, creates an instinctive desire to know more about the concepts of education.

In all likelihood the best method to gain knowledge on learning is through reading books or using other media to further explore the subject.

For many people, the phase of being competent and conscientious is the most crucial one. If you're interested in getting the most out of your brain, you should thoroughly study the books that deal with this subject. You are already aware of the theories which are essential to this.

Two instances of this are evident in the above paragraph:

* Differing between informal and formal learning

Understanding the different roles that individuals play in taking on the role of an entire group

The paradox is that the process of learning makes it difficult to stay curious in it, without putting this into use. Similar to this it is difficult to master the art of the architecture. It is possible to learn about the way houses were constructed during the Middle Ages, although it isn't necessary to design and build a house. Although you're not required to put your theory into reality, your curiosity is there. It's not the case when you are learning.

It is necessary to get a direct experience of something before you can truly absorb the concept. Learning from a book to be a better person instead of doing it will eventually frustrate you. You'll probably like to use the information that you've accumulated in your daily tasks.

Different types of learning

The idea of learning is broad enough that it's straightforward to translate it into other areas. and yet, we fail to take note of the different methods of learning. Imagine a typical day in your daily life. You must figure out the amount of different experiences you have. For each subject you can think of an example of at least one. Review all the knowledge you've gained from the this month.

*	Formal--attending a university, registering for an educational program

* Informal--observing a person whom you admire conduct a conversation with your family members centered around your thoughts on a recent film

* Temporary--trying out a brand new computer program to create new shelves, which are in a flat.

* Permanently-dealing with an emotional moment, and apologizing for any wrongdoings

Externally certified--getting an award for saving lives and completing an MBA

* If you are interested in learning how to install tiles in your bathrooms, or creating an edifice in your garden.

* Obligatory--to attend a course that you didn't choose and obtaining an education

• Voluntary: choosing to browse the web, and learning to speak French

* Social--learning how to play games as in a group, and then launching on a new project along with colleagues.

* Individual - reading an ebook, or browsing the internet.

Many have found that of the ten types, the component in "informal" learning include the most elements.

Chapter 5: Choosing Your Way

We've put in a significant amount of time revising and enhancing our overall goals. This is just an excellent place to begin. Then we can begin the actual task of digging to the depths of the subject and choosing the areas to concentrate on.

Micro-Goals

Micro-goals can be beneficial to your mental well-being. They can take huge and daunting goals and reduce them into something achievable. Imagine this in the following way that having a well-defined goal which are evident in our refined Goal inventories are a crucial stage to begin. It helps us determine where we're going.

Let's say that you'd like to learn to play guitar. For a beginner, this is an extremely broad goal and, as soon as you start you'll feel depressed every moment you realize you're still not able how to play guitar. It's much better to limit your goals. For instance, you might want to master five chords as well as the blues scale or even your first song. These are all more achievable objectives and you'll be able to be able to achieve them quicker if you keep your eyes on these goals. When you achieve each you will be able to create a fresh achievable goal. Before you realize it, you be able to play guitar.

For a more personal scenario When my first baby was born I felt overwhelmed. My son was due and I would be the one the sole parent throughout his life. I'd be required to educate him on how to be a decent person. Be sure to protect him. Help him develop the social skills that can help him throughout his future life. Find him the best schools. Help him avoid making the same mistakes I've made in my own life. It's huge. However, only if you view it this way. The error I made the one I think that a lot of new parents make, is that I was too focused into the issue.

When I became a father the responsibility was exactly what I had envisioned. There's nothing more overwhelming. The reason I was able to bear it and did not make me crazy due to stress, was because every day, I have to accomplish small-scale goals. They're often fairly simple. You've got one of your children. It's your responsibility to be in charge of the child's wellbeing for at least until the time he reaches eighteen , and probably more than the age of eighteen. What do you have to do? Make sure that the baby is fed. Change the diaper. Do a pat on its back. Speak to it. Try to smile. In terms of micro-goals, they aren't too bad. It's not that intimidating in the right way.

I'm not attempting to dictate the way you run your business. It's not with the concept of self-directed learning. But as a learner/self-teacher, you'll need to figure out how to get from your refined goal to your daily micro-goals. There are a number of ways to achieve this, but I would like to encourage you to discover the one that works best for you. Start using your Refined Goal Inventory as well as Learning Map, then breaking it down into micro-goals. It's probably wise to start with the master list of goals to follow as you progress. It is possible to formulate this in chronological order or in a different method, maybe visually which is based upon your Learning Map. But if this is what works for you, then you could establish your daily goals for learning at the conclusion of the day. Review the places you're at and where you're required to take your next step.

Based on the way you prefer organizing your work It could be a good fit for your style of organization. If you prefer to be flexible, rather than rigid, and nonlinear instead of linear, this flexibility could keep your learning experience interesting. In reality, what I'm speaking about is left-brained and. thinking with a right brain. Left-brained thinkers, the rational people who are detail-oriented, will do effectively with a full outline from the start. Right-brained thinkers may prefer some flexibility and flexibility to make adjustments mid-course by setting the day's learning objectives at the conclusion of the course. The main thing to remember is to determine the best way to learn for yourself.

Chapter 6: Enhancing Memory

In this article I'll go over methods to increase the capacity of your memory. It is important to keep in mind that a particular method might be more effective to you than other methods, therefore it's best to experiment with different methods until you find ones that are effective for you. First, I'll discuss a few small tricks to help increase the power of your brain.

Your brain will get a exercise.

As with muscles, the brain is likely to decline if you don't exercise it on a regular basis this is why it's crucial to give your brain stimulation every day. The most effective brain exercises are those that challenge your routine and push you out from your comfortable zone because these workouts will build new neural pathways and strengthen your brain. A good brain workout will provide you with a new skill. If you train your brain through doing things you're skilled at, you're not working in any way. The exercise for the brain must be challenging and you must devote your entire attention to it. The workout should not be something that you can perform without putting in a full mental energy. It is best to have a skill that you could improve on. Try to find brain exercises which allow you to begin with a basic starting point and gradually increase your level. Always strive to test your metal abilities to their limits. If an activity seems to become too simple, it's time to move to the next stage. Be sure that the brain exercise is rewarding. The reward system is an excellent method to gain knowledge. The more you're interested in a particular sport and the more you be engaged and strive to make improvements. Therefore, it's best to select an activity that you enjoy and are looking to improve your skills with. A great brain exercise doesn't have to be an intense game like chess, though that's a feasible alternative. Learning to play guitar, dance, or speak Spanish are all viable alternatives to providing your brain with a stimulating exercise. The most important aspect is that it can stimulate your brain, and you are enjoying it.

The brain isn't just the thing that requires to be exercising. Your body too needs to be exercised. Studies have proven that exercise is vital for the health of your brain. It boosts the amount of oxygen reaching your brain, and decreases the risk of diseases that cause loss of memory like diabetes. The reason you should exercise regularly if you wish for your brain to be in top condition is due to neuroplasticity. Regular exercise has been shown to play a crucial part in the formation and expansion of connections between neurons. Find activities that stimulate your heart, such as aerobic exercise. Exercise after waking is an excellent way to begin the day and build your brain to learn during the course of your day. If you're taking breaks from your studies to go out for a walk, or do a couple of jump jacks. It's possible to find an exercise routine during breaks can to reduce stress and mental fatigue, so that when you come back from your break, you'll be rejuvenated and ready to study.

Make sure you get enough sleep. Adults should get at minimum 7.5 hours of sleep in order to keep from becoming sleep deficient. Even a small amount of sleep could negatively impact the performance of your brain. If you are sleep-deprived and unable to think, think, remember and solve problems, as well as be creative decreases dramatically. Sleep is crucial in the field of the development of memory and learning. Research has proven that sleep is crucial for brain growth and for the development of neural connections. When you are in the deepest phase that you sleep brain's activity levels are at their highest since it is during this time that the majority of new neural connections are created. Set a schedule for your sleep and adhere to it. You should go to bed at the same hour and rise every day at the exact time every morning, even on the weekend. When you're doing this, you'll be less tired in the morning , and you'll be asleep more quickly than you're used. Do not check your phone before going to sleep. This may be to be a challenge for a lot of people, since checking your smartphone before bed is a common habit for many people. However, studies have shown that the blue light produced by TVs, phones and computer monitors triggers chemical reactions which inhibit melatonin. It is an hormone created from the pineal gland which regulates wakefulness and sleep. Do you find it difficult to let go of your phone while you sleep? The majority of phones nowadays come with a feature to reduce how much blue light that is emitted through the screen. It is recommended that to not use your phone before sleep, if your want to use your phone, make sure that you enable this feature. Do you drink lots of coffee? It's a good idea to reduce your intake when you're having trouble sleeping. Some people have a great tolerance to caffeine and sleep well, however it's a tiny percentage of the population. If you believe that you are having trouble sleeping because of caffeine you can cut back on it and see if this can help.

Socialize and have fun with your friends.

Humans aren't isolated creatures We thrive on social interactions. Interacting with others is among the best exercises that you can perform to improve your brain. Research has shown that having an enduring relationship with others isn't just beneficial emotionally but also crucial for the health of your brain. Research conducted in researchers at the Harvard School of Public Health has revealed that those who regularly socialize are the least likely to suffer memory loss. Social interaction aren't limited to interactions with animals, but human interaction can be beneficial to the health of your brain. Being with your dog is a great way to exercise your body, which means you can kill both birds in one fell swoop!

Stress can cause havoc on the health of your brain and is often linked to memory loss. Chronic stress has been found to cause brain cell death and to damage the hippocampus area of the brain. It is the region of the brain that is used to create and store memories. To reduce stress, it is important to establish realistic expectations. Don't be stressed trying to achieve the impossible but instead, achieve your goals each step at a time.

Make sure to take breaks regularly. It's crucial to know the time you require breaks. A lot of people think that it's not productive to take a break however this isn't the case. Actually it can boost your productivity because it gives you the chance to refuel your brain, which means that when you come back from your break and are back working at your best. Do not keep a journal of your emotions. The act of expressing yourself is a fantastic stress-buster. If you are storing negative thoughts in you only makes you feel more less stressed. Giving thoughts to someone else can relieve all the stress from your shoulders and make you feel more relaxed because of it. Avoid putting yourself through the paces. Make time for yourself so that you can focus on the things you'd like to accomplish. The best way to approach it is to be aware that you live to live, not to live for work. Concentrate on one thing at an moment. Be present in the present. Do something and doing it with ease, without distractions, no pressure or burnout. When you focus on one project, you'll be more focused, and your productivity will rise and you'll be exceptionally proficient at the job you're doing. The notion that multi-tasking leads to greater productivity is an illusion, it just makes it appear like you're doing more.

You'll notice that you'll be less distracted and less likely to delay your work If you stick to the one daily task. Studies have shown that mediation can be beneficial in relaxing stress. Meditating is linked to reductions in anxiety, depression and diabetes. It also lowers blood pressure, and increase focus, memory and concentration, as well as learning abilities. Meditation has been found to modify the brain. Brain scans of people who meditate on regularly have been found to show increased activities in the prefrontal area of their left which is the part of the brain that is associated with emotions of joy. The research has also revealed that the the cortex of the cerebellum is generally higher than those who do not meditate, resulting in more neural connections as well as the development of ability to learn and memory.

Many people believe laughing is their most effective treatment, and that's certainly very true! The act of laughing activates multiple brain regions and results in greater stimulation of the brain and more healthy brain.

If you are listening to an impromptu joke you're trying to determine the punch line. This stimulates the regions of your brain which are linked to creativity and learning. An effective way to bring an extra dose of laughter into your daily routine is to begin laughing with yourself. Don't avoid sharing embarrassing experiences within your own life. Reviewing the times you thought were stressful and finding humorous side of it is an excellent method to boost your mood and let yourself relax. Spend time with those you like being around. People you can connect with and who bring you joy can make your day more enjoyable. It is said that laughter can be infectious and so be around those who have a lot of fun and you'll be sure to have more laughter in your life.

Take in the foods that your brain loves. The exercises for your brain aren't the only thing to aid in improving brain memory and a healthy diet could as well. Research has proven it is true that Omega 3 fatty acids can aid in improving the health of your brain. Foods that are rich in omega 3 fats are usually cold water fish , such as tuna and salmon, sardines, mackerel, herring and trout. Even if you're not a big fish lover omega-3 fats can be present in seaweed, walnuts, flaxseed oil and squash seeds, spinach, and soybeans. A diet rich in fruits and vegetables may also boost the health of your brain. Fruits are loaded with antioxidants that shield your brain cells from harm. As you get older it becomes harder for your brain cells to defend themselves from the highly reactive elements called free radicals. All cells in the body makes unstable oxygen molecules. You're also exposed to them by the environment via air pollution. If unchecked, these free radicals harm cells via the process of the oxidative stress process, which is believed to be the primary reason behind the onset of age-related metal-related illnesses. The body fights off free radicals by generating its own anti-oxidants.

Therefore, help your body by eating more fruit that contains lots of antioxidants. Another way to gain the most antioxidants into your body is to consume green tea. Green tea is a source of polyphenols, an effective anti-oxidant. Not just do they protect the brain from damage caused by free radicals but they have also been proven to aid in fighting cancer and reduce inflammation. It might sound strange but alcohol has been proven to aid in improving cognition and memory, but excessive alcohol consumption has been proven to kill brain cells which can accelerate the decline in the brain. It is best to stick with the wine or grape juice in moderate amounts. Red wine is superior to white wine since it's high in resveratrol a flavonoid that increases blood flow.

Health is an important factor when you want to live an enjoyable life, and there are a variety of diseases that can cause memory loss. Therefore, it is important to determine any health issue you suspect you may have as quickly as you can so that you can lessen the effects. The presence of cholesterol and high blood pressure has been associated with a decrease in cognitive capacity. If you've been diagnosed with one of these conditions, be certain to speak with your physician. Numerous over the counter medicines have been proven to hinder clear thinking and decrease memory retention. This includes allergy and cold medication as well as antidepressants. While I'm not suggesting you discontinue taking these medicines but it's important for you to understand their impacts in your brain.

Chapter 7: Building Reading Skills

Elon Musk believes that "it is feasible for everyday people to make the choice to be extraordinary." This is a development that begins by reading. Reading is an essential ability. This is particularly important when you're a student since the ability to read quickly and comprehend the content you've read will prove useful. If you'd like to read as fast like Elon Musk, here's an article that can be used for more efficient and comprehensive reading.

It is important to realize that reading isn't necessarily linear. Humans read by jumping as well as "saccadic moves." Every "jump" concludes with you fixing your attention on the end in the book you've been reading. If you're not well-trained the fixation could take as long as quarter of one second. The duration of fixation even if it is under a second should be reduced.

The second is that humans have a habit of going back, or rereading the lines after reading them. This can consume up to 30%

of your time spent reading. Like the pause that follows each saccadic movement, the regression is also to be avoided.

The session will be split into three sections. In the first, you will be taught how the technique is used. In the second, you will understand how to use the technique. Thirdly, you'll learn how to test your skills using comprehension tests in reading.

For this test the objective we'll concentrate on is three times the speed you normally read at. For example, if you're reading 300 words/minute, and you would like to increase this to 900 words per minute, you'll need to work on reading at 1,800 words per minute.

The Baseline

The first step is to establish your current reading speed. For starters, lay your reading materials flat on the reading surface. Take note of the words on those first 5 lines. Divide these words by 5 each, and you'll have your average of words per line.

Then, you need to count the paragraphs of text that make up five pages. Dividing this amount by five. Then, multiply the number of words on each line you saw earlier. With this equation you will get the number of words on a page.

Note the first line, and then keep track of your time as you read at a leisurely speed for about one minute. Keep in mind that you're not just looking for speed, so you should read at a pace that lets you comprehend the content you're reading. After a minute, multiply the amount of lines you've read by the number of words for each line you read earlier to determine your wpm.

Tracking

It is the next stage to monitor how many regressions you have. To achieve this, you'll require a ballpoint pen. Place the pen in your palm with the cap in place. Draw a line beneath the text you are studying, keeping your gaze at the top of the tip. This will ensure that you keep up your speed and will eliminate any possibility of focusing as you work. In the beginning don't be worried about your reading comprehension.

Then, you can practice using the pen tracker. Start reading for about two minutes. Concentrate your eyes at the pen's edge while you read. Make sure that each line is about one second. Then, you can begin growing your speed of reading when you switch through one page one page to another. Keep reading however, whenever you can do not take more than one second for each line. Don't worry about the level of comprehension.

After you're finished, repeat the procedure, but this time allowing yourself three minutes of time to read and ensuring that your pen stays in the line for two and a half seconds.

Continue to do this until you are no longer using the pen.

Continued Practice

When you reach the moment where you don't require the pen to direct you, the second step to begin reading without comprehension. Repetition the process using the pen and try to comprehend words while reading them and then increase the speed of the speed of your reading to don't need using the pen.

In order to ensure the outcomes you are hoping to attain are realized, you should continue to be reading throughout your day. devoting minimum 1 to 2 hours of concentrated speed reading time each day. Always strive to improve your reading speed increase. Always monitor your progress with your timer and keep up the exercise for at least up to three days.

Determining the Results

To see if you're succeeding with this modification then mark the first line again , and begin reading for a minute, but this time at the speed you can read with the fastest comprehension. Then, evaluate the wpm you reached in this test to the wpm you had when you first started.

If you follow the correct procedure in the first week, your wpm will increase significantly.

Chapter 8: Surround yourself with the Right People

Another aspect to take into consideration when you are studying is the need to study on your own or in an entire group. Many will say that the best way to concentrate on what that you're studying is to do it in complete silence. Some argue that the energy and support of other people can be crucial in keeping focused on the task that is at hand. Also, people react to specific environmental elements with different methods, therefore there's no definitive solution to this issue. The key thing to consider is determine which environment work best for you. Then, you can hope to boost the outcomes of your research efforts and increase the amount of information you can master in less time.

When you are studying in a group, there are a variety of factors that need to be taken into consideration to ensure you benefit the most from your energy and time. The first step is to ensure that the group you are studying with is a good match for your individual requirements for studying. As we have discussed in previous chapters, you might discover that you need to be in a quiet space while studying, or you may prefer ambient sound. The time of day and location you are studying in is crucial for how efficient your studying sessions turn out to be. If you plan to study alongside other students then you should be sure that they fit to the categories that will benefit you. It is not logical to work with a group of loud people when you require quiet for concentration. Furthermore, it is devastating to be studying with an entire group of people who are unable to stop eating food while studying since this could impede the outcome of your effort. So, even if you decide that joining groups is a beneficial option for you, it is essential to find the perfect group that meets your requirements. Being with like-minded people can make a huge difference in aiding you in learning anything faster and efficiently.

Another thing to take into consideration when you are studying with an entire group is the motivation. Certain groups are highly driven to learn and concentrate on the topic that is being studied, while others may be more relaxed, opting to study alongside having fun. It may seem like an easy choice to make. What if you be wrong in choosing the ones who are totally committed to learning and studying? The reality is that a study-only group could be a bad choice depending on what energy fits your personal style. The group's energy is the most important factor when choosing an academic group. Students who are solely focused on schoolwork can lead you to feel more stressed during your studies, because they do not allow you to blow off steam in the course of studying. If this is the case, a group that blends working and enjoyment could be for you. You want to be at ease and secure as you can while studying, so the group has to aid in that feeling in a meaningful manner. Making the effort to play with various groups can help you discover which one is most suitable for your needs.

One trap that a lot of people get caught in is to believe they are spending their time in more intelligent people is the proper choice. For certain people, this may be the case however there is much to be gained from having a conversation with others of similar intellect, or even less intelligence that you. For those that are comparable to you in terms of intellect, they will usually encounter similar problems and issues similar to those you face. Therefore having a chat with those around you can be extremely beneficial as it can help you to solve the issues that you encounter with other people who are in the same boat. In addition, you might be able to offer assistance to others due to having overcome similar issues previously. It is true that those who are like-minded can make any issue more manageable by sharing experiences with the same viewpoint.

Being around people with a lower level than you may be extremely beneficial. Although it may sound counterintuitive initially, there's actually an extremely rational reason for this concept. If you are studying with someone who are less knowledgeable or educated about the subject matter than you, you'll be able to help them comprehend specific things. If you can answer any questions that they pose, this allows you to apply what you've learned. In teaching others, you'll improve your understanding of the subject. This will allow you to better absorb the latest information you're learning. If you spend a lot of time with others who are more knowledgeable than you, and you feel like you are constantly trying with the pace. Instead of being able to answer questions, you could be the only person asking every. This is not a good way to go about learning since it does not give you the opportunity to apply your knowledge to use.

Chapter 9: Visualization Techniques To Improve Your Memory

When it comes to increasing the power of your brain and preparing it to be more efficient Visualization techniques come to the rescue because they involve you in the experience and help your brain to focus more on the content and efficiently process it.

If you're looking to learn the poem, or an operation that is statistical or commit that difficult client list or speech for future reference, visualization can assist you with the task.

Here are a few efficient visualization strategies that you can employ for testing for your own purposes:

Visualization & Association Technique

People retain information better through visual aids. However visual aids don't always require an external surface but they are inside your brain as well. If you are able to perceive images in your brain's eye, you are able to improve your cognitive skills and make use of your brain to the very best of your capabilities.

Images are usually concrete however, the information we receive is largely abstract. Visualization and associations techniques can help transform that abstract data into simple to comprehend and process mental images. Mental images are used as mental hooks that aid you in removing the information you need from your mind.

The brain processes information from visual sources around 60 times faster than it can process text. About 45% of the nerve fibers connected to the brain connect with your retina. This means that visual images comprise approximately 95% of information that your brain receives. This shows clearly that your brain's neural pathways favor processing and storing information from images over simple text.

The techniques of visualization and association allow you to concentrate on crucial information, form mental images that are connected to it, then form connections that relate to it in order to embed the concept in your brain.

Imagine that you wish to remember the name and the types of stratovolcanoes, which are mountains that have sharp tops. To remember the name stratovolcano you can make use of the name in itself to make a mental image and create an association with it. For example the word'strato is pronounced like'straight oh which is why you can create an imaginary picture of the mountain and visualize the words'straight oh" emerging from it, as scorched lava. This will create a fascinating picture that will stay in your mind , particularly when you are able to focus on it for a long time and visualize it in your mind.

You are able to create any kind of mental image that you want and make any connection to the data you want to keep in mind. It is important to create a captivating mental picture , and then make a more exciting connection with the data that the image acts as a hook in your mind and will help the information stick to your brain. If you follow this method correctly it will embed that information in your memory for the long-term. The most important thing to be able to access it at any time is to remember the connection often.

Name face portrait

This amazing trick is closely linked to the technique of visualization and associations and is extremely effective in retaining names and remembering them swiftly. If you struggle often with remembering people's names , maybe because of a lack of memory or because you encounter many people each day This technique will be the knight of shining armor.

It is necessary to create an image of your face of someone who's name you want to recall and then make an amusing mnemonic based on the name of the person. The next step is to create an connection with the name memory as well as the snapshot of your face and then focus at it for quite a few minutes until it becomes a part of your brain.

For example, if you've just had the pleasure of meeting 'Owen Soloff And you want to remember his name since you wish to remain in contact with him and grow your connection into something that is significant, you can use this technique to learn his name and even his face.

Owen recalls Owen Wilson who was a well-known actor, so it is easy to imagine Owen Wilson's face in your mind. Pick any distinctive feature of your friend Owen Soloff, say his large, blue eyes as you picture Owen Wilson having big, blue eyes that pop out of his eyes as the actor swoops around and continuously sings the word "Soloff" with a hilarious accent.

The entire scene will be replayed in your mind for a few times, and then think of your new friend's smile every time you remember it. In just a few minutes, you'll have formed a strong link between the whole image as well as the face of the person and be able to recall his name when the next time you get to meet him. Repeat this process whenever you need to recall someone's name or face, and you'll eventually impress others by recalling their name after only one interaction.

Engage your five senses in the experience

Visualization is most effective when you use all of your five senses of imagination until it is alive. Imagine yourself licking choc chip-flavored ice cream off of a waffle's base on a hot summer day. The delicious flavor would begin to ooze in your mouth when you imagine eating that delicious sweet. It is then possible to imagine the way that the waffle cone will feel when you hold it in your hands, as you feel the cool twirl on your hands as it melts before it drips off. In just a few seconds you'll be transported to a different world of delicious ice cream that makes you smile.

That's exactly what visualisation does to the mind: it transports you to a different world and helps you remember the things you are focusing on. If you want to understand and store something in your mind visualize it, and then create an entire scene around that information. You can then use your five senses during the sensation.

Imagine the various sounds you could hear as you walked by Concentrate on the taste you experience, imagine feeling various textures, focus on the smell of any scent you detect as well as take note of the things you see all around you.

As explained in section 4, visualizing when you engage your senses stimulates various brain regions that work in tandem to store different kinds of information and add it into your memory for the long term. If you can think of the scene frequently, you'll be able to recall it in the event of need.

Memory Palace

This innovative visualization technique alerts your brain to the point that it are able to remember lengthy and complicated bits of information, such as speeches cycles, presentations, formulas and long sequences of names.

It is as simple as having to think of a place that might be real or imaginary , and draw a map of the same location. Then, you must find interesting locations within the area to write down the information you want to remember and then walk along this route a few times until it is ingrained in your brain.

Here's how to try it out.

Consider your home as an imagined palace or any other location you love or one that you are drawn to. The more strong the connection you make with it the more you'll be able to recall it and all the details that is associated with it.

The next step is to choose the route that you would like to go through. If, for instance, you imagine your home with an entrance and a rear door and you would like to access it through the front door, choose this and then determine the areas you'd like to go. You can pick a couple of rooms and corners or explore the entire home. The length of the journey may be long or short according to the information you'd like to remember and also your own personal preferences.

Take that path at least a couple of times and be sure to make the exact turns and corners, rooms, and nooks on each occasion to make it a permanent part of your brain.

Once you've completed the course and can visualize it in your mind's eye Think of the information you'd like to remember. If you're able to form any funny associations with any part of information, you can create rhymes, or if you have the ability to make an acronym that you can remember quickly, try it. Repeat it several times through your mind, or read it aloud when you are doing it.

After the associations have absorbed into your brain, explore your memory palace and select out various places to save some data. For example, if your entrance has a mailbox and you want to make use of it to recall the first sentence for your talk, you can throw those sentences inside. Then, you go inside and you will find an ornamental planter on the right side . You could add some additional sentences. So, you can keep going along the route you have chosen and add several sentences or bits of information you would like to remember in the selected location. It is advised to talk the information out loud when you are memorizing it in order to permanently commit it to your memory.

It is suggested that you stroll along the path, stopping at each spot you've kept some data in and then go through it several times to ensure that the information is firmly ingrained in your brain.

Once you've committed the route and all the necessary information in your mind, the only thing you have to do is envision your place of memory and write it down. it. When you are traveling on the path you've chosen you may stop at certain spots and be able to recall the information you have memorized.

After using that information, you are able to dispose of the memory palace or store it for any new information. In the case of a presentation, for instance, when you've given your presentation you are able to eliminate the memory palace and construct an entirely new one to help you remember some other thing, or utilize the same memory palace using the same method or fresh method to recall new details.

Use this method every when you encounter a difficult detail you'd want to keep in mind It will always work for you.

The next chapter will discuss the techniques for sensation you can employ to increase your brainpower.

Chapter 10: Notes Duly Taken The Foolproof Method for Notes that include both physical and mental Notes

If you attended school, you were anticipating the day you'd start taking notes during the class. Maybe you had the opportunity to try this out as a young kid, and you improved your abilities the older you became. But the more notes you made and the less interesting the notes got and the less you were inclined to take them.

When you went to college (or in the event that you did be a part of life in the world) you used a basic note-taking method however, it's a mess at the very least, and you realize that your notes won't be able be able to help you navigate any serious scenario.

This doesn't just lead to frustration and anger, it also makes one wonder why it is worth not taking notes at all in the first place. In the end, what can you gain if you write down something on paper, only to glance at it but have no idea what it's about when you look it up later?

If this sounds like you do not worry it's not a problem for everyone else. Many people would like to remember more things, but when they attempt to make notes to help them remember they are left with more stress than they started with.

Why?

The reason is that the notes users take aren't sufficiently broad. They're too focused only on one specific aspect in the course (or business conference, etc.) and fail to consider additional aspects of information that might help (such as the context.)

This is why I'm going to teach you how to efficiently note notes, both written and mental. These will take notes which are concise but will keep your mind occupied when you're required to assist you in carrying your assignment before you.

Step 1: determine what's important about the information you're taking note of. Step 2: decide what is important about the information you are taking note.

In an office meeting or type of class for academics It is easy to get overwhelmed by all the information being handed to you and begin recording everything that could be significant for you in the near future.

At the end of your engagement, you've many notes in which you may be able to discern some meaning from the notes, but then you realize that you've forgotten why you recorded something or how it's pertinent to the work you're doing now.

Instead of scrambling to write down every sound that is important, consider what the true, fundamental importance of what's being discussed or taught. If the information can truly help you in the future, note it down. However, when it's just some interesting data or something else about the subject matter that was brought into the mix to help you comprehend it, then don't bother noting it down.

Step 2: Write the information down. Include why you did it.

In the same vein of selecting what's important enough to take note of and what's not, it's crucial to write down why you made a note of something whenever you take notes of it.

We've had the experience of learning about something or planning for something and glancing over notes only to look up something that is important, but we have no clue what it is or what it is discussing. This causes more stress and the more stress you put on yourself and strain yourself, the more difficult it will be for you to concentrate on what you have to master or do at the moment.

If you weren't just to record the things you want to keep in mind and include a brief explanation of the reason you recorded it this will significantly simplify the task of trying to understand yourself when you look back at your notes later on.

For instance:

"Always select the one to the right."

This sounds like a very important note that you'll want to keep in mind. After a long week at school or at the office, looking back at your notes, you might not be able to comprehend what the note is about, which indicates that it did you no good.

It could be like this:

"When wiring an automated copy machine, begin by cutting the wire that is on one side."

Which one do you think is likely be more effective in the near future?

The issue in taking notes and the method by which many people make notes is that they do it quickly, and without paying attention to what was actually spoken or the notes they make. Note taking does not have to be a stressful experience and doesn't need to be done in a chaotic manner. Approach note taking with the same confidence you would any other task and you'll be aware of what you wanted to convey.

Step 3 Step 3: A is to B , as the subject is to what?

If there's one thing that scientists can be sure of regarding the human memory and brain is that the more we are able to connect things with one another in a way, the more likely will be able to recall what we need to remember.

Have you noticed the amount of times the children are taught colors by association?

A red apple.

The sun's yellow.

A blue-sky sky.

Black dog.

The children are trained to associate a color of something they recognize as related to the color. This is a method which is utilized by those who want to learn several languages.

Similar to this you can apply this method in your personal daily life to give yourself the same benefit of being able to remember things. This is useful for reading information and the verbal communications you use.

Below is an illustration of a fantastic method to remember your name. In the end, we are all apprehensive about forgetting names of people when we've just met the person, and it's the most common occurrence.

For instance:

"It's great to meet you, my name is Ted."

"It's nice to get to know you as well. Tell you, Ted you're doing. What's the thing you're doing."

"Oh I'm taxidermist."

Here's a scenario where association could easily be a factor and make it much simpler for someone to recall Ted's name.

The first is that alliteration can be employed. It is possible to use T as well.

Ted The taxidermist.

or, a more circular approach can be used however, with the same outcome:

Ted is taxidermist. Taxidermists make trophy animals. Bears are prize animals.

Ted the Teddy Bear.

How do you accomplish this?

In terms of the process of association it boils down to the way your mind operates. There are those who opt to use brief and concise comparisons, and then there are those who prefer long and drawn-out comparisons.

In all times, it's an established method, however it's not a simple black and white approach which you have to follow by a particular way. Instead, try it out and method and learn how your brain functions.

Then, you can move on to the next step by in a position to make connections between your everyday items in your daily life and also the latest items you hear or read about. Similar to the other components of learning accelerated it is a technique that will be difficult to learn initially However, with time it will become an automatic process.

Chapter 11: Learning Techniques

Each student is unique. Certain students lucky sufficient to possess photographic memory remember everything they see, even though they view it one time. Some learn more efficiently using visual aids.

One of the most important aspects to put the power of accelerated learning to work for you is to discover the best methods that match your own personal style of learning. The more you know about your brain's capabilities and how it learns, the more able you will be in figuring out the techniques which are most likely to lead towards success.

To keep this in mind In this chapter, I will discuss a variety of methods of learning that can aid you in adjusting how you learn.

Sensory Reinforcement

Human beings are blessed with five senses: sight hearing scent, touch and taste. The majority of classrooms, however only use only one or two of them at the all times. Actually, the two most commonly used are hearing and sight.

It is definitely possible to master the subject without using all five senses, however the more you involve your senses during the learning process the greater chance you are to learn new information and keep the information for later use.

Let's consider a straightforward illustration. Imagine a college student trying to understand basketball. If all the student receives is a basketball lesson and basketball, he'll have no idea of the sport at the very least.

Imagine that your teacher shows the student a film of a basketball match. The student can experience what he's learned in real-time. He might have a better knowledge of the process of playing.

If the teacher gives his student basketballs it is possible to feel the weight and feel of it and smell the materials that was used to make it and even try an appreciative bounce, or pass.

The person who has the chance to take their basketball outside, master the move and dribble and even play a few games will have a better knowledge of basketball than one who simply listens to someone else talk about it.

Each of these examples highlights the value of reinforcement via sensory. When you master something and experience it in action or get the chance to apply it, your brain is trying to connect all the information you've learned. Each aspect of the learning experience - the auditory as well as tactile, visual and physical - is built upon the previous.

Some topics can be a good candidate for this type of learning faster than others.

Here are a few examples of how you may be able to integrate these subjects:

If you are studying a certain subject and you're not sure if you know what you're studying, try visiting YouTube and see if you are able to find an explanation video that can help you understand.

Do the things you read make you think of a song, a book or an event? Consider the reasons. Listen to the tune. Look up pictures to help you write down your knowledge to your memory.

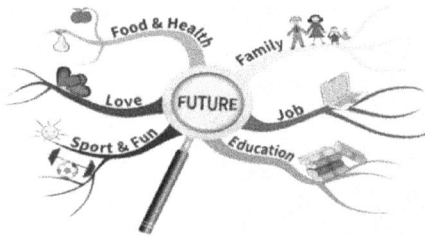

One subject in which students embrace the idea of using sensory reinforcement is the study of foreign languages. Teachers in this field frequently present films, instruct students in songs, and ask them to perform dialogues that incorporate words used in the classroom. They might even let students taste traditional dishes to enhance their education.

The benefit of this strategy is that it stimulates your senses in a holistic way and provides your brain with an array of memories to refer back to when recollecting the lessons you have discovered.

Active Recall

Human memory is unreliable. What you are exposed to most often is what will most likely to recall as you search your brain for facts.

One way to help students to excel can be active recall. It focuses on the regular recollection of facts to improve the brain's capacity to retain them.

One study saw students pair with each other to learn the new vocabulary of a foreign language. The study group students were tested with flash cards. When they were able to recall the word correctly the word was added to their flash card collection. Also, every word was reviewed several times.

In the group that was controlled students were asked to remove the them from the cards after they were able to recall them. The results indicated that students who had access to the information they were learning frequently - the second group - retained about 80% of the words they had learned in the following quizzes, whereas the control group only remembered 30 percent of the words they were taught.

The key takeaway here is that repetition can be your best friend. The more frequently you come across the same piece of information the more resonant the neural pathway to it will become.

In reality, just going through your notes on a regular basis is not the most effective method to learn any subject. It is important to mix spaces of repetition with more active methods discussed in the book.

Do What You Know

One of the most effective methods to speed up your learning is to share the knowledge you have acquired. If you are responsible for someone else's education then you are responsible for their learning.

to dissect the information into a coherent manner. The process will ensure that you fully understand the subject.

Even even if you don't have any willing students If you don't have a willing student, you can apply this method by creating an outline of your lesson in the same way as if you had to instruct the subject. What would you do? What topic would you discuss first? The thought of these questions could aid in filling in areas of your knowledge that aren't covered and take a topic to an entirely new level.

Make use of Mind-Mapping

Mind-mapping is a visually-based learning method that helps you simplify complicated topics to be able to recall later.

Start by creating an symbol or icon on the middle of a page to symbolize your primary issue. After that, draw branches from it to include subtopics as well as related topics. For every item that you have on your mind map sketch a tiny image. Conceptualizing images to convey ideas, and linking subjects to subtopics assists you in putting the knowledge you have learned in the context of.

If you've got some strategies for learning now is the time to move on to the next step. In the next section I'll explain how to design an effective study plan to help you overcome difficulties in learning.

Chapter 12: Clear Your Mind

Being overloaded and mind can be difficult. Being a hyper-active mind can lead to anxiety, which affects your mood, learning capabilities physical and psychological health, more. When your brain is scattered and you're not sure what you should be focusing on, or more important, you begin to be aware how your performances at school, work or at home begins to decrease and you feel like that you're unable to function anymore.

There are many ways to keep your mind off studying, reading, or writing however, before we dive into the various ways learning can free the mind of distractions, we should consider ways to cleanse your mind every day and get rid of that cluttered mess that has engulfed your brain!

The first thing you must do when you're feeling overwhelmed is to speak to someone. Be it your closest acquaintance, a stranger on an anonymous hotline and even an therapist talking to someone has been proven time and time again to relieve stress and let things go from your mind.

Sometimes, keeping things inside can create more stress than you started with which can push you to the breaking point that can end in a disastrous way. If this happens, you're creating your own stress. All of this could be avoided if simply chat with someone.

A diary also has assisted many people! If you've got a journal or diary to record your thoughts in it, it is as if you are letting your emotions leave your body through your hands and onto paper. A lot of people write in their journals regularly, and use journals on a regular basis. The people who write on a daily basis have many books in order to demonstrate the dedication they have to write their thoughts and emotions down. What are you waiting for? Why not take a chance?

You can also relieve stress by engaging in a distraction. If you have things to complete all day long it is impossible to think about events that have taken place, things that could happen, or events that are likely to occur. The thought of pondering your issues is nothing more than a waste of time and time that you could spend unwinding and relaxing, until you discover a way to fix the issue you're facing.

Exercise is among the best ways to reduce stress. If you are able to put all your anger and frustration in a box it's like you feel tension levels diminishing with every punch and kick. Every activity you perform at the gym typically serves a reason. When you go on the run, it's generally to think or let your mind go. Training for strength and kickboxing are commonly used to help get you out of your frustration. There's an exercise for everything, I swear.

Long, slow walks in a tranquil setting is something you must consider doing. I suggest you find a pond or lake close to you and heading for a long stroll near the water. Nature sounds are proven to soothe the mind of many. Many people find it helpful those who are struggling with sleeping.

In terms of sleep, anxiety and mental clutter can result from sleeping disorders. It is crucial to get the right amount of rest for many reasons! I can't say it enough! Sleep is crucial to your mood, learning capabilities, and energy. Without enough sleep, you're likely to be overwhelmed exhausted, cranky, and tired!

I'm aware that I've discussed the practice of meditation within two chapters however, this is a different option to calm your mind and relieve stress. When you practice meditation as I've previously mentioned the objective is to relax and be able to forget everything happening in your hectic life for a few minutes. All you need to do is find a spot that is comfortable with your eyes closed and pay attention to your breathing or the beat of your heart. Give it a go and let us know what happens.

If you realize you're in need of some distraction because of the noise that has engulfed your mind Perhaps some work is just what you require!

Many people believe that reading books is enough to take them away from their normal lives as they're transported to a place that is free of stress to think about. In the realm of Winterfell there is no one who is getting ready for combat. When you're taken to Saint Vladimir's vampire school there is no need to worry about who is going to learn the truth about you. You'll get to see others deal with stress which are far more difficult than yours.

Reading can be more than an escape from reality, but it can also be an opportunity to examine your reality, regardless of whether you're reading a novel. It is often apparent that the issues you're facing may be much worse, even if the problems you're reading about are fictional. It is crucial to recognize that no matter what issue you're confronted with, somebody else may have it more difficult. This also gives you the opportunity to test your speed reading abilities!

It is also possible that some of the methods that we have discussed in previous chapters may help in finding a peaceful space. For instance, you could sit on the couch with a jigsaw. Puzzles can help you focus by allowing your mind to wander and allowing you to shift your thoughts back to something peaceful and tranquil.

A crossword puzzle could be a good idea! When it comes to reducing stress any activity to distract you from the stress and anxiety of daily life is something you should consider doing!

It's always about your individual preferences, what's happening in your life and why you need to relieve stress. It could be that you need to get away from a specific person and/or your parent. This could mean going to a place that you would not normally go to.

Chapter 13: Creating good habits to boost your Memory

Sharpening Your Memory

After you've sorted out your routine for the day and have a plan for your day, you can start changing your life more. The suggestions below have been tested and proven to be helpful to anyone, no matter if you're a:

* Student

* Parent

* Work part-time or full-time

* Director of the Company

* Retired

Are you looking to improve your brain.

This is a manual intended for everyone who wants to succeed in their lives. The only thing you need to do is apply the tools that are within your capabilities. There is no financial investment required to invest your time.

Things you should have already been incorporating into your daily life:

* Home-cooked food

* Eliminating or at a minimum, drastically decreasing, the amount of sugars, carbohydrates and processed foods.

* Performing at a minimum the most basic weekly workouts.

Plus If you've accomplished all of these the above, your sleep pattern will be healthier.

If stress starts to show up in your life, take a break and do some relaxation exercises. Breathing techniques should be an integral part of your daily routine and so will relaxing your muscles, as I've demonstrated in the chapter 2.

How do you define Memory?

The next step to getting to your goal of faster learning is to increase your memory. Anybody with the proper attitude and determination can boost their memory. Even those who resort to excuses, like:

* "My memory is not great and it will never improve."

* "I'm too old."

* "I'm too busy."

* "I don't have time to bother you."

* "It's just a bunch of garbage."

* "I'm not smart enough."

What's the deal "I'm glad to inform you that the things I mentioned above mentioned are nothing more than inadequate excuses!"

There's no reason to believe that you can't enhance your memory, regardless of your level of education or profession. While you will never be able to achieve the ability to take photos however, there are things it is possible to enhance your recall of the day-to-day. Through our memory strategies you'll be able to develop the ability to concentrate. This will lead you to be better at your work and overall well-being.

Let's look at that very powerful organ called the brain. Particularly those neurons that we mentioned earlier. They are neurons and brain cells which form your brain's communication network. The brain's activity relays all the information you can smell, taste and feel as well as learn every day.

Your brain makes a decision about whether the new information you've learned is worthwhile to keep or not. If it's worthwhile it's then stored in your long-term memory. If not, it's kept in your short-term memory. It's short-term, meaning it's information that will be removed and forgotten once it is are no longer using it.

The brain's memories stored in the long-term memory banks can be brought back when needed. Through the same pathways of neurons involved in storing memories, the data is able to be retrieved in a new. This storage method doesn't function as a photo, which is able to capture every aspect. When memories are recalled and recalled, it could be somewhat blurred or unclear. This is why you can't completely depend on memories.

The aging process can weaken the neurons, which means that the system isn't working the way it once did. However, this can be fixed since the brain is a massive muscle. It's your responsibility to build it up so that it can function more effectively.

A very crucial ways to learn new knowledge is your memory. If you don't know how to make use of your memory to the fullest extent and then you're not really learning new things. The brain will think it's useless information, and retain it in the short-term memory. If you do have an excellent memory recall, you may possibly acquire a variety of new abilities. It's essential to develop your memory abilities. Then, you can begin to think about accelerated learning as a thrilling way to move forward. When you improve your memory you're training your brain to become more efficient. These kinds of exercises will increase the number of neural pathways. Then, you can accumulate more knowledge, which makes your mind sharper.

Mnemonics

Name of the Goddess of Memory in the language of ancient Greek was Mnemosyne which means "remembrance." The old Greek term "mnemoniks," means "related to memory." These words have evolved into the current term of Mnemonics. It is the study of improving our memory.

Mnemonics are ways of linking cues, images, or abbreviations that assist us in remembering large amounts of information. These are some of the most common mnemonics that many are familiar with:

* "I" before "e" but not after "c." It is of of course, this isn't 100% accurate however it is a good general rule of thumb to follow for spelling.

This is a method of remembering the exact word that is spelled twice however, it can mean two things. "A "principal" at the school is your"PAL." While"a "principle" that's something you believe in is a standard."

One way to keep track of the location of the points on the compass is to spell in the words "NEWS" in the "S" design. N (North) located on highest point. E (East) located on the left. W (West) located on the right side and to the on the opposite side of E. Then, S (South) to the lowest.

As you will see, they aren't completely foolproof. Alongside using the standard versions, you can create your own to ensure you'll be able to remember more information.

Billy always wrote"restaurant "restaurant" wrong. He put it in his notebook with the spelling "restarAUNT." The issue was that he was unable to distinguish the word's ending with two spellings "aunt" as well as "ant." The word was one of the words that threw him off like it happens to anyone. To help remember the correct spelling of "aunt," or "ant," at the end of the word, he informed him that every time you thought of dining out, he'd compare it to bugs. From that point on, he was aware the word's ending was spelled "ANT."

Mnemonics have a wide variety of ways of interaction. They have proven efficient for memory retention. However, you may need to memorize an entire poem in order to remember something that is factual for instance, the dates in the calendar:

30 days are September March, June, and November

The majority of them contain 31 minus February .

It has 28 plus one extra in the year of leaps.

It's the kind of rhymes you learn as a kid and keep it throughout your life. Many people still utilize it to remind themselves of how many days are in the month.

Mnemonics are often more complicated than these basic examples. You could even make use of images, like in this biology-related question that you could find on the exam papers:

* Question: Name 3 depressant drugs.

The answer is Barbiturates, Alcohol, and Tranquilizers. In this case, the initials are BAT. If you faced this question on your exam you might be able to remind yourself to imagine the bat.

Mnemonics can be created in various varieties:

* Letters with patterns, like acronyms

* Short phrases

* Images

* Numbers

* Poems

* Charts

* Songs

Do you recall the ABC song that you may have when you were a kid so you could master the alphabet? This is a method that can be utilized at any stage of life. When you learn the order of a simple phrase, it can be used to lead to recalling the sequence of planets. There's even a whole song to help you remember all 50 states of the USA. What a useful device Mnemonics are.

Loci Memory Palace

There's an alternative and powerful mnemonic technique that can increase your memory. It is also among the oldest techniques for memory, called The Loci Method. It is sometimes referred to as the Memory Palace, Mind Palace or it's called the Memory Journey. It's believed that it originated in it's origins in the Roman Empire which is often called the Roman Room method. It is a method that only uses one space and the things inside the room. Loci is an Latin word that means "Places." This is precisely the thing you'll need if you decide to employ this method. In order for this method to be successful, Loci method to be effective it is best to make use of a place you have a good relationship with, for instance, your home.

It is possible to use any structure so long as you are familiar with the design.

To start using the Loci method, you have to visualize each aspect of your selected area. That includes the design of the structure and the items like furniture, ornaments, as well as images that are displayed on walls. It is vital because every object is connected to the information you wish to recall. Let's go through an Mind Palace Journey:

* The goal is to connect the information you have to remember with a specific part of the structure you've selected.

Step to the entrance, and associate the first memory you wish to remember to the front door. However, it isn't enough to only link the memory item to the door. You can further develop this by imagining something new in the memory as well as the door. For instance, if you must remember a specific date for a train ride and you can imagine a speeding train that is crashing through that specific door. Imagine yourself walking through your "place" connecting memories to objects. The more vivid the image you have in your head the more likely to be able to recall it. We recall only the bad ones and not remember the positive ones?

As you enter the door, think about the hallway. There may be coat hooks and mirrors in specific locations.

* Connect more information to each image and every piece of furniture you go through rooms. It is possible to have every room with a distinct motif of memory. This is a great option if you're learning about different subjects.

It's a lot of work and exhausting. It will take time to build the memory castle. Concentration on the subject is a key factor in establishing the memory connection. It is then necessary to focus to recollect the information in Your memory's palace. Do not expect it to occur in the course of a single day.

It takes practice, but believe in your capacity to master it, as it's been proved to be effective. Clemens Mayer took home his World Memory Championship in 2006 with the help of an Loci Memory Palace. There were 300 stop points during a trip around his home. Each stop was a memory for him to remember.

If you can master it and it is working for you, there's no reason to not be in multiple "place." Each one can have various sets of information that you must remember. Imagine the possibilities for your job; it is truly mind-boggling to think of the lengths you can go with this technique.

Chapter 14: Strategies for the Pareto And Pomodoro Strategies

This chapter you'll discover two strategies for advanced learning to help you master difficult subjects easily The Principle of Pareto Principle and the Pomodoro Technique.

Pareto Principle

The Pareto Principle, also known as the 80/20 Rule, states the notion that 20% of an effort should result in an 80% return. This principle can be applied to any subject or discipline that you would like to master in a variety of fields, from literature and business to engineering to mathematics and much more.

The idea was formulated by a man called Joseph Juran who was inspired by the Italian economist Vilfredo Pareto (hence the name). Pareto found out that, in the year 1906 all Italian land was owned by only 20% of Italy is owned by 20 percent from those in the Italian population. Pareto also found that 20 percent of the pods of peas produced 80% of the total amount of peas.

The 80/20 rule and the Pareto Principle can significantly impact your capacity to learn. To discuss the issue Let's consider language learning as an instance. If you are using this to learn of new knowledge, you must think about the words you select to learn as well as using will be the most important objectives. For instance, focusing on learning the top 100 frequently used French words will result in an increase of your French proficiency. The importance of focusing on the fundamentals is vital since you might not be able to master a vast vocabulary or an extensive understanding of French grammar to know how to write and communicate in French.

The language and vocabulary you select to concentrate on when you wish to acquire a new language should be something you can employ in your native language. There are instances when the language training focuses on obscure content to aid in encouraging the understanding of cultures. Language training should instead be used as a way to discover a particular subject or to learn about a discipline. Additionally, the majority of people give up studying a foreign language after the lessons get boring or monotonous.

To help make the language you are learning more meaningful, you must consider the reason why you're learning the language. This is an important consideration. Learning the classics of French and reading classic French novels is not helpful if you have be employed in Paris as engineer.

It's also a good moment to study the basic principles of grammar in a specific language. The language training that focuses too much on the vocabulary is not beneficial for those who wish to become fluent. Once you have mastered the fundamental grammar, you must learn to use the language in conversations. The fundamental understanding of 20 percent part of the language (grammar) can allow you to beat the other 80percent of spoken language (conversation).

Pomodoro Technique

The Pomodoro Technique was developed by the Italian Francesco Cirillo in early the 1980s. The timer used in his kitchen was that resembled the shape of a tomato (pomodoro in Italian) to help those who need to cut down on tasks into 25-minute intervals, or pomodoros. This approach is based on the idea that regular breaks can boost mental agility that is vital to learning.

How to Utilize the Pomodoro Technique

Follow these five steps to make the most of this technique. Pomodoro Technique:

Choose the lesson you'd like to complete (write an essay or read a chapter from a book or chapter, etc.)

You can set the Pomodoro timer for 25 minutes.

Make sure you exert all your efforts and mental energy into your job until Pomodoro is over

Pause for at least five minutes

Start the timer once more and continue to work until you've completed four Pomodoros. If you're still not completed, go back to work and take a break of 5 minutes between breaks.

Be sure to record when you have completed a the pomodoro portion. This will help you increase your peace of mind and will also experience the feeling of accomplishment when you complete things. With this approach you will be able to easily understand how to identify the tasks that must be accomplished or perform your work in a more relaxed setting, and break down the task or task into smaller but manageable chunks.

Exercises

Always remember the Pareto Principle whenever you're studying difficult topics. Many find it beneficial to print large signs with the words "Remember 80/20" and putting it up on their workspace. This way they are always reminded to adhere to the rules.

You might need to purchase an omodoro timer, pen and a notebook to track your progression. There are programs and apps that make it easy to utilize this Pomodoro Technique.

Chapter 15: Determine Your Baseline

Before you try any of the strategies described below, determine your current reading speed , so you are aware of the speed at which you read . Then, check your speed before using the strategies. This will allow you to track your improvement.

To do this, open any book you want to read and look up the words within the first five lines of each paragraph. Divide the total amount by 5, and you'll find the average amount of words per line. For example 60 words on 5 lines would twelve lines of words.

Now , take note of the number of lines across five pages. Divide the number by five to obtain an average of the lines within one page. Then, multiply this number by the number of words you have calculated earlier, and you'll have the average word count on the page. Start with on the line that is first, then switch to a timer for one minute, and read it at the normal speed. When the timer rings it will stop. You can then divide the lines' number by your average number lines or words to calculate the number of words that you've read in the time of a minute. Record the number in a notebook and then follow the steps below. Try each one several times before you determine your amount of words in one minute.

Stop Sub-Vocalization

Sub-vocalization is an adolescent practice in reading that hinders your ability to learn and read quickly. It's the practice of saying every word you can think of as you read it. If you choose to use sub-vocalization, first you speak the word to yourself before hearing the pronunciation. It takes longer than it takes for reading a sentence, because you're performing two tasks that is reading the word and the second is focusing on the pronunciation. But, if you stop then you can go from one word to the next and then to the next without thinking about how the first word is resonating within your head. This can save time, allowing you to read the entire article in around 30 percent less time.

To become a speed-reader put a stop to sub-vocalizing words within an article while you read it. To achieve this you can try these suggestions:

First, you must acknowledge the voice inside your head that reverberates each when you read. This recognition is essential as it is the first step in getting rid of the voice. Pay attention to your reading style by slowly reading 300 to 500 words article or entire piece. If you are unable to pronounce each word while reading it, you're probably in the problem with sub-vocalization. If not, good!

After you have acknowledged the voice that is in your head, say to yourself "I will write one word after another without subvocalizing." Do this several times with a firm conviction. When you repeat this idea repeatedly and with conviction then you confirm it in your subconscious mind, meaning you believe that it is accurate. This makes it easier for you to subconsciously follow this advice and become aware of the voice that is within your head, so that you are able to consciously silence the voice whenever it gets louder.

Each time you sit down to read, repeat this affirmation several times until you are conscious of the work you're going to be engaged in, and pay full focus to the task in hand.

After that, you should begin by reading through the content and take your time reading each word and without subvocalizing. It takes just seconds for a single word to be read. when you're done then quickly move on onto the next one to ensure you can resist the urge of subvocalizing it.

Repeat this several times with one piece . Then do this exercise for at least four to five times a day to train yourself to not sub-vocalize when you read.

To overcome the habit of subvocalization, it is a process that requires lots of repetition however, perseverance and persistence will help you get there. Once you've beat this habit, you'll discover yourself reading around hundreds of words 30 seconds or less.

Overcome Regression

Another bad habit of reading that will slow the speed of your reading is called the process of regression. Regression is reading a text repeatedly, without a valid motive. If you are unable to go back to a section of text you just read, because you have forgotten the information you read or want to make sure that you have did not miss something it is a sign that you're practicing regression.

Regression can cause you to lose the flow and structure of the text you're reading, which reduces your understanding of the topic, requiring you to take longer to comprehend the content. Here's how to stop this habit.

The first step is to be aware of any activity you perform. If you're reading do your best to be engaged in the process and pay attention to it only. Regression happens when your mind is lost in thoughts. Naturally, if your mind is elsewhere, but your eyes are focused on a page it is likely that you will be distracted as you read it, and you'll likely read it over and over. Be aware of the content you're reading can help to concentrate on the text. This allows you to read each word in complete concentration and avoid reading the text over and over.

To pay attention to the content you're reading pay attention to each word you read and then say, "I am focused on studying right now" at least a couple of times before starting to read anything. Your mind might wander to think a few times. Every time this happens, gently announce, "thinking has occurred" and then return your focus on the content. Repeat this process a few times until you are able to establish an habit of reading with attention and not fall back into relapse every when you go to read.

Keep a pointer or highlighter on your person and use it over every line you go through it. You could use a pencil or pencil, your finger or another object as a pointer. Your eyes will follow the tip of the object, assisting you avoid reading the content. After you've broken the destructive behavior of regression, you can begin moving your pointer quickly over every line you read it. The more quickly you move your pointer, the more quickly you'll read.

Skim and scan the Content

Scanning and skimming through any content will save you a lot of time reading. Scanning and skimming help when you already know of a particular subject and require to read it quickly to review the information you've learned. But, if you're studying something to you for the first time and you need to go through something in-depth it is not recommended to scan it. However, skimming can be an effective skill that can help you read text quickly and boosts the speed at which you read. Here's how to learn it.

Take a quick look at your chapter outline or the table of content in the book, thesis report, or any other huge content to identify the most important elements you have to review.

Choose a few chapters or content depending on your requirements to read. For instance, if , for example, you have to write a report on the project you're working on, you should read its outline and research so you will have an overview of the work you've accomplished and avoid getting a crucial point off.

Look through the principal headings of your selected chapters and then read the highlighted image or information or content in bold or italics as it's likely to be important.

Check out the beginning and the final paragraphs because they are the introduction to an important topic and provide a conclusion to the paragraph.

Read the summary or conclusion of each chapter for an overview of the material.

Do this every time you need to go through the text, review the important points and get grasp of what's going on in a group, so that you have a brief overview of the topic and talk about the subject.

Enhance Your Eye Movement

Many slow readers suffer from inefficient eye movement. Inefficient eye movement means that you concentrate on just one word you read and then move through each line in a piece of writing. The process of reading each sentence slowly, and in a single, sequential manner is beneficial when you are practicing mindfulness and improve your focus. Once you've achieved this level It is now time to enhance your eye movement and increase its efficiency.

Effective eye movement enhances your peripheral vision which makes it easier to read a large block of words in one go, without having to read each word separately. If you read a large block of words at the same time you read a single word, you'll be able to be able to read more quickly and learn things faster. To increase the speed of your eye movements you can do these things:

You can relax your gaze when reading. Relax your face as you read and extend your eyes to the entire line, instead of just one or few words. As you ease your eyes, you'll begin to see blocks of words together, instead of seeing each word as an individual entity. Being a pro at this requires a good amount of time and practice. As consequently, be patient while you try this technique.

When you are at the conclusion of a sentence, let your vision peripheral to dominate so that you can quickly read the words that are left. It is a part of the vision field, which is located just outside the center of your eye. The picture below illustrates the vision field as well as its various components. A clear peripheral vision is when you are able to discern the nooks and corners of any object and are conscious of what is happening around you. For reading, active peripheral vision is when your eyes are able to read words faster which allows you to learn and comprehend information more quickly.

Take a look at these hacks and keep practicing them over and over again so that you'll improve your eye movements and your ability to read quickly. The most important thing is to take the time to master each technique and repeat it until you are comfortable with the concept of it before you move on onto the next step. This will improve your ability to recognize patterns and stop the focus from switching from method to the next.

While you are applying these strategies, you should also focus on improving your capacity to absorb information and remember it to improve your overall ability to think. The next chapter will show how you can do this.

Chapter 16: Focus

There's a notion that's been floating around for a long time which is counterproductive that in order to be productive it is essential to be capable of multi-tasking. This isn't the fact. One of the best sources I've come across that disproves and discredits this mythological notion is the one of Cal Newport's Deep Work. The idea behind this book states that you must constantly work at extremely high as well as productive rates. In order to achieve this, one Newport's primary methods is to be focused on the work that is in front of you, whether that's writing a book, preparing an incredibly life-changing pitch or pursuing a course. His book points out clearly in a scientific and logical manner that multi-tasking is not just unproductive, but is the most detrimental factor to maximum productivity, particularly for tasks that require a lot of concentration.

It is not necessary to go through the entire guide to reveal the myth of multi-tasking and demonstrate this fundamental principle. Instead, I'll just give you the basic concept.

The Multi-Tasking Myth

It's true that there's nothing like multi-tasking. The term was invented due to the rapid growth in the computing capabilities of processors or computer chips beginning with the Pentium processor line from Intel, Inc. in the early 1990s. It's apparent to the untrained observer that computers are able to handle multiple operations that is, tasks at the same time. Think about this while I'm downloading an enormous digital item that I bought recently, as I'm working on this novel using my MacBook Air with the Microsoft Word software. The MacBook's background appears to be I'm also using my Pomodoro Timer app (more on this in the next chapter) It gives the impression the laptop could be working on three tasks simultaneously.

However, the truth is that It's not. It's performing one task at a given time, and switching between different tasks.

However, due to the extremely powerful processor in my MacBook it is able to switch between tasks at astonishing speed that it seems to my slow-perceiving eyes that it's completing all three tasks simultaneously. If our modern computers aren't able to complete multiple tasks simultaneously, what's the reason anyone think that we could?

You might be thinking, "Hey, jugglers are capable of focusing on several items at the same time. What is the reason they're adept at juggling bowling pins, balls or Molotov bombs effectively?" In response to your question, I'll tell you that they're still focusing on one thing at a given time, switching between them in a rapid manner, much as your computer. In particular, jugglers are focused on catching and then swiftly throwing an object in a particular manner and in a specific direction to make the catch easier it again and to avoid collisions with other airborne objects. If a juggler can juggle three balls using one hand, what they're doing is concentrating upon throwing, and then catching just one ball at a given time in order to ensure to ensure that no one of the balls drop on the floor.

The Multi-Tasking Effects

Multi-tasking, as it is understood in the full sense is a serious issue that can result in two negative consequences. The first one is negligence. When you're juggling multiple tasks simultaneously by switching between them frequently the chance of being negligent is significantly increased. Consider, for instance the danger of the danger of texting in traffic.

You could argue "I am not in danger of getting into an accident since when I type, I put the phone right above the steering wheel, and within the direction of the road in front of me. If anyone or any vehicle comes across over, there's no way for me to be able to miss it!" In response, I'll say, "Believe me, been there, done that and have nearly paid a huge cost for it!" If you put the phone in direct line of sight from the roadway, you're focused on reading or writing an email, which takes your brain from the principal work in front of you. In addition it reduces your and focus down to the dimensions of the phone's screen on a computer, making all other things in you "line in sight" virtually unnoticeable.

To see a more clear image take macro photography photos that show objects of a smaller size like a coffee cup is sharp and large-than-life in the foreground. However, the the background appears blurred. It is true that texting while driving could make you more reckless and increase the risk of causing an accident when you suddenly encounter someone or something that comes into your path.

When we talk about speedy learning, the principle of avoiding carelessness is also applicable. What will you gain from trying to study or learning something new if you're not fully focussed on the task at hand? If what you're trying achieve is quite difficult to master then you'll have to be extremely concentrated, and focused. You shouldn't not pay attention - or to be unable to grasp a vital piece information quickly or not completely understanding, keeping the information and storing it for later use.

Another possible consequence of multi-tasking, and the most pertinent to learning speed can be that it interrupts mental momentum. What exactly do you mean when I say this? Let me use a different driving analogy.

When you've been in in a car particularly one with a manual transmission and you'll be aware that the fastest method to go from point A to point B is although it's not actually straight, but it's something similar - to travel forward with a minimum or any stops. While it's obvious, here's the reason why: when you stop often, your vehicle loses its momentum and has to move again from the point of a complete stop. This takes more effort and time. The energy and time you expend are lost.

From a teaching perspective interruptions during your study disrupts your brain's momentum. How? By interrupting your thinking process. If you're at the point G on the way to point Z in your subject of study that is accelerated Stopping to complete something else will force you to retrace your steps in order to locate the place you stopped. The disruption as well as the necessity to go back and trace your steps within your thought flow will add valuable time to your learning process.

In this moment I'm sure I've made a compelling case to you to think about sharpening your focus when you are learning something new, and trying to learn at a speed that is faster. If you're clear and focused you'll soon realize that the speed of learning is accelerated compared to the normal pace of learning is a given. If you're not, get willing to accept the slow road as the only option.

Practical Tips to Improve Focus

First thing that you'll have to accomplish is getting enough quality sleep. Coffee and energy drinks in buckets but you'll be unable to make them as effective as getting enough sleep. This alone can make those energy drinks ineffective (except maybe for the flavor that coffee has, which I am a fan of!).

Quality Sleep

How do you ensure good quality sleep? The following suggestions have been useful in my quest to always (not completely) have sufficient quality sleep

All devices should be turned off at least one hour prior to going to bed. The light from the television and other electronic devices and the stimulating effects of watching content via these devices could make it difficult to fall asleep quickly.

There is no coffee or caffeinated beverage until 4 P.M. Although some people are immune from the negative effects caused by caffeine many aren't. Don't risk it to risk your health - it's not worth it.

The lights turn off or down. The brain interprets the light as a signal to get up and remain awake. I find using an eye mask beneficial to ensure that I sleep in complete darkness. sleeping. It also lets my brain slow down, relax and sleep even when there is a light in my bedroom (perfect when you have a roommate who is awake longer that you).

Temperature control. The heat can prevent the body from sleeping enough to sleep or get a good, restful sleep. The reason animals hibernate is in winter, it's because it's cold! A cooling system can be an excellent investment in providing a consistent, high-quality sleep.

Drink a calming elixir for sleep. This was something I heard from Tim Ferris' (bestselling author of the book The Four-Hour Workweek) audiobooks. Mix with 1 Cup of water that is hot, one tablespoon of honey and 2 tablespoons apple cider vinegar (preferably Bragg's). I'm not sure exactly how it works, however it makes me sleep more deeply and awake refreshed every day.

Another aspect that has allowed me to control my own "monkey brain" and improve my concentration has been mindfulness meditation. It's not difficult to see that the practice of meditating every day for at minimum 10 minutes has allowed me to develop my mind. I'm able focus on a particular concept for prolonged period of time, similar to as a marathon runner capable of training their body to run for long distances over long periods of time, something that the majority of people don't have the ability to do.

I employ a specific breathing method I learned from another popular writer, Mark Divine, writer of The Way of The SEAL and Unbeatable Mind. The technique is known as"Box-Breathing" Technique And here's how you can perform it:

- Sit up straight and comfortable on a stool;

Close your eyes and put the hands of your legs on them.

- Relax your entire body;

Breathe in by letting your nostrils open for five seconds and fill your belly with air, and then your chest.

- Breathe five seconds.

exhale all the air through your chest, and then off your belly in 5 second intervals;

You should hold your breath for 5 seconds, then repeat the breathing pattern for at minimum 10 minutes.

A word of caution: particularly at the beginning, it can be difficult to track your breathing because thoughts will flood your brain. This is the monkey brain working. Don't be a jerk whenever that occurs. When you realize it, just return to your breathing rate. Return each time you notice thoughts disturb your thoughts. The trick is to acknowledge the fact that thoughts are forming in your head, and then allow them to go away as quickly as they are acknowledged. There's no method to master this and it's all about persistence and consistency, just like training for the marathon. As time passes you'll reap the benefits of a more energised and concentrated mind that is better able to meet your needs to learn faster.

The Pomodoro Technique

I'm sorry for using a different running-related metaphor. My friends who have the ability to complete full marathons each year are adamant about the Galloway Run-Walk technique for training. The method was created by a person known as Jeff Galloway, the Run-Walk method is one in which a person is able to run for a certain number of minutes and then walks for a specified amount of time. The most widely used run-walk protocols are the intervals of 3-1 and 4-1, i.e., run for 3 or 4 minutes , then walk for a minute. The walk break is not negotiable.

The reasoning behind this is quite simple The reason for this is that runners don't have to wait until his legs are exhausted to rest in this manner, thus reducing the time frame for the development of muscle fatigue significantly. In this way runners' muscles are able to maintain optimal performance for longer, and even perform faster in general.

The mind too is an muscle, but an emotional one, and can be prone to fatigue, too. Therefore, it could tremendously benefit from a mentally-focused variant of the Run-Walk technique that is known as known as the Pomodoro Technique.

The Pomodoro Technique makes use of thirty to 35-minute working cycles. Each cycle consists by 25 minutes intensely focused work (in this instance studying or learning) then a mandatory mental break of five minutes. Every 4th cycle the mental break can be increased to 10 mins. Note that the break is required. You'll be tempted to extend it, but resist. You'll notice the difference after a couple of days of exploring new ideas in this manner.

You might ask, "But didn't you just talk on the value of having mental momentum and concentration?" Yes. It's true that it's not an interruption in focus, it's just an opportunity to relax, and an extremely short one at this point. When you're not doing anything that requires a large amount of focus in your brief break, you'll never lose your momentum. It's similar to the Run-Walk approach in that if you prolong the walking time to 5 minutes your muscles will begin to begin to cool and you'll be feeling slow and sluggish. By limiting your break to just one minute, you give yourself the opportunity to take a break without having enough time to get cool and lose speed. Try it! You'll see.

Feel the heat

When cooler temperature are beneficial to help you sleep however, they won't enhance your capacity to process information faster. Focusing on something while in a cold atmosphere is likely to allow you to relax to the point that you're asleep (and being cold can cause you to lose focus). And I'm sure we are all aware of how difficult it is to study and learn when we're tired. This isn't a good idea.

This isn't to suggest you do your work in saunas. I'm simply saying that should you have some influence over the temperatures in your learning space, you should exercise it. If you aren't able to adjust the temperature in the room, then you should regulate yourself by wearing clothing such as a jacket or sweater. This could also be the case for you, in the event that you are prone to becoming restless in a warm climate. Make sure you are aware, and be sure you adjust your environment to ensure the best performance.

Stop using the internet

One of the drawbacks that comes with being connected to the internet is the overload of information at the point of being distracted. With the ease with that we can be informed and communicate with others and be contacted, it's becoming increasingly difficult to concentrate on things. That's why I stay offline whenever I have to study or do something. If I'm in need of good old the Mr. Google for research, I try to log out of my social media accounts or email addresses. If the subject I'm studying and working on becomes important, I turn off my mobile and put it away to not be distracted by texts or calls. I've designated three "online" times throughout the day to reduce distractions at a minimum, and to maximize the focus of my time at 10:00 a.m. and 12:00 p.m. as well as the hour of 4:00 p.m. When I get home at 5 p.m. It's time to study because my work or workday is finished. My friends are used to this.

Give yourself the benefit of the doubt by going "off-the-grid" as well as offline while you are learning or working on something new.

Music Only

A lot of people are listening to music while working or study as do I. However, I've realized that not all music is equally effective in focusing.

The best music to learn from are ones that don't have lyrics. Why? If you are listening to a track that has lyrics, your brain will immediately seek to understand the lyrics either by following the music or guessing the next word. This is multi-tasking. Music that is purely instrumental of popular songs has similar effects. Although they may not contain words, however the tune is familiar and can trigger your brain to fill in any gaps using the words. This is also multi-tasking.

Even when I play instrumentals, I would not recommend listening to a lot of aggressive such as fast-rock guitar, club music or dub smash. These types of music are too stimulating and could become distracting rather than helping. Pick a tune that is a part of your surroundings, helps keep your mind clear and your mood sane and does not cause distracting factor.

Personally, I consider classical guitar, jazz, and classical piano with a moderate pace to be excellent listening or studying music. I find them to be relaxing, and not lulling me to sleep. Have you tried these? They might help you too.

Chapter 17: Photographic Memory

It is impossible to conclude the process of learning accelerated speed without talking about the significance in the photographic memory. Photographic memory is also referred to as an eidetic memory which involves the ability to recall numbers, names, images or words with lots of accuracy.

To be able to learn more quickly it is necessary to develop your memory so that you will be able to remember important information that is going through your brain. The idea behind"photographic" memory is that it "Photographic" memory is it's similar to an image within your memory bank. You can access images as well as content out of your memories.

You are able to view the image at any time you want to zoom in on it, or even share the content with others. We all have a memory for photos that lets us see the things we've seen all over again.

We must improve the capability by being aware of it and growing it even more. As an example, for instance, you could recall a specific street you've walked down or a location you've been to before when you are asked.

A memory that is photographic is an asset for anyone who is keen for speedy learning. As you progress you'll need to remember a number of previously taught lessons to enable you to stay consistent with your understanding.

With a memory that is photographic it is possible to learn to accomplish something new without using the information you've already learned. When you are learning you will also be able to grasp the aspects and concepts, the steps to take as well as colors, along with other aspects of learning faster.

Different brain regions change in different ways and the time of adolescence is an important stage in the process of changing. At that point when we begin to build an acute memory, however other factors can also affect the process.

A few of these are genetics, brain development and personal experiences. The things you do every day affect your life in a positive way.

This book will assist you to determine your photography skills and make use of them by demonstrating ways in that you can develop it completely.

Be more vigilant

The most effective way to improve your photographic memory is to be vigilant. Do not simply observe things, but see them as they really are, and incorporate into consideration. If you are eating lunch, try not eating the salad on its own and also take note of the different colors of vegetables. Make sure to take in as much information as it is possible to remember about the establishment and the surrounding environment.

If the time comes, this will be a memory in your memory and if someone asks you what you were eating to eat for lunch two weeks later you'll be able to answer. Even if it's difficult to remember the specific nature of the dish, you'll still be able to use the word "Salad" due to the fact that you're extremely attentive when you ate lunch.

People who are successful often depend on their memory to reproduce the same pattern that worked for them previously or when they had a previous contract. You'll also be an asset for your organization because you are an employee with an image memory since everyone will depend on your unique techniques for speeding up the process.

Note patterns

Another method of giving your memory in photography a boost is to study patterns. Systems lead to full structures, therefore, if you are aware of the trends in a certain ability or concept, you'll be creating photographic memories.

How do you make an authentic Watermelon Cocktail? You purchase the watermelon, extract the juice, then you get all the ingredients (based on the flavor you prefer) and then you prepare your drink.

You don't have to be able to recall all the steps. If you could make notes of the first patterns, you'll be able to master the technique anywhere and at a speed that is incredibly fast.

The next time you're looking to create the perfect watermelon drink, keep in mind the glass, watermelon and every other action will be in your mind.

For other jobs that have more complex designs, don't fret about what you can accomplish. Divide the process into groups, take an image of them and store them in your memory.

Practice remembrance daily

In this book, we've stressed the importance of practicing since it is the basis of learning that accelerates. The more you practice , the more proficient you will become. The same principle is applicable to developing memories of photography through the act of remembering.

When you were a kid, you were promised a present, you remember. You also made sure the person who promised you the gift kept it otherwise, you'd be crying and throw temper tantrums.

As an adult you likely cannot remember what was occurring to you since you don't take the initiative to develop your knowledge by remembrance.

If you wanted to learn how to build an automobile in the factory, you'd need to be practicing remembrance in order to complete the task faster than what you expected to take. The process of joining a car is similar to doing the same thing over and over again, with only a few changes.

If you are able to remember the steps in one car, you'll become an expert by when you put together the next car. It is easy to remember things with an image memory, and there's an opportunity to test this from something you do every everyday.

If you are in taxi to head home at night, and the driver makes the wrong route and you are unable to tell which path isn't the right one to follow? It's because you have an image memory (subconsciously formed) of the way that leads to home.

Recalling the past, you need to improve your skills until you become very proficient. Because of the significance of memory in our entire conversation We will guide you through strategies that work for recollecting

1. Keep an eye on the subject matter you are studying

If you're not interested in the knowledge you gain it is possible to forget about remembering anything from it. Everything you learn should be interesting to you, particularly if it's something you're compelled to know.

The pursuit of interest increases the likelihood of memory!

It is easy to recall the things that interest you. This is why before you choose an ability that requires accelerated learning make sure that it's something you enjoy.

2. Connect what you have learned with your knowledge

Everything you're learning right now will be in some way linked to something you've already learned earlier in your life. Therefore, by connecting them, you'll create a pattern within your brain.

This is a way to recall one thing whenever another idea pops into your mind. For example, if are learning to play an instrument, but previously played another organ before, link both playing experiences to create a.

You must remember the basics of playing one instrument to learn how to play both. The universe has a link between what we learn and everything else we do discover it, look it up and apply it to improve your memory capacity to increase your memory of photos.

3. Make bedtime your time of the day.

The time at night before going to go to bed is a good time to practise remembrance. However, you need to be in this manner in order to make it succeed.

As you prepare to go to bed, don't just simply go to sleep. Do your best to remember what you've learned in great detail. When you do this, you're creating images of it for your memory.

Even when you're asleep you'll find that you are able to dream about the thing you were thinking about because it's stored in your mind. Consider the time between bed and night as an opportunity to build your memory capabilities.

4. Be aware of the little things that can lead to greater things.

If you are trying to improve your memory skills, begin by focusing on the simpler things before moving on to the more complex things. For starters, think about your food, clothes and friends, birthdays, and anniversaries.

In today's world it's not easy to remember things we have planned. However, that's the reason accelerated learning is about: helping reach what others consider to be "Impossible" or "Difficult."

Get started today; keep in mind your child's favorite friend's name. Keep track of what you ate in the morning and your boss's wedding venue and all other things that is important to you.

If you do this regularly it will help you be able to keep in mind those important details that run across your skills, work and even lessons.

5. Recall your memories even in a noisy environment.

The majority of people find it easy to remember and recall everything as long as the surrounding isn't too loud. But that's not the "Average" scale. It is important to go above that since it's simple to forget when everything is calm.

But if you must remember a specific detail in order to accomplish more quickly and are in a noisy area What are you going to do? And, most importantly, if you are able to remember something you've experienced in a noisy setting this indicates that the concept that you've etched on your mind will last forever.

Therefore, start today practicing by consciously stepping out of your home base. When you're with your friends at a gathering be sure to check your mind and the thoughts you've acquired.

The more you are able to recall what you've hidden away in the back of your mind , in non-traditional places The more you build the memory.

Create a memory palace

Do you recall what you had for lunch two days ago or even yesterday? Now , you're scouring your thoughts trying to remember whether you can remember. It is a sign that you possess the ability to remember photos, If you don't have any, you're not the only one.

Many people don't remember their home phone numbers in addition to not having a look at the mobile phone. A majority of adults have difficulty trying to recall the birthdays of three or more people in their family.

Many people are unable to remember more important details than the food they ate at lunch. You can remedy this problem and improve your memory by creating an memory palace.

If you've got an impressive memory and a memory palace, you are able to recall easily your activities that you participated in prior to that, including your experiences in learning.

A memory palace can make things easier for you to use it's similar to a hard drive that within your head that you can access to download data. So let's say you've developed an app for a business and two companies would like you to do exactly the same thing but in shorter time frames.

Instead of being overwhelmed by the taskat hand, all you need to do is return into your memory castle. Take the information you require from the data you've accumulated.

You'll be able finish each task in record time as you're not relying on manual direction no longer. You're relying on the information that you've saved about how you developed the app in the past.

In the past what was the method used by people to navigate around towns and cities without signs or Google maps? They utilized the same technique of building memory palaces. How do you create an memory palace?

The first step is to make a space within your head which is secure for the exact information you wish to keep. The palace may be your office within your mind or even your residence. You must contemplate the space with great detail since this is where you create memories.

Then, you create the images that represent things you need to keep in mind often. Choose objects that stand out with your activities such as bright colours, vibrant colors, and particular objects.

Within your head, step to your dream palace and set the items you want to store there. It is important to do this by visualizing yourself unlocking the door to your memory palace and then storing the information.

After you've completed this take a break and keep your attention for a few minutes. The reason for an extra moment of distraction is to see whether the data stored in your memory palace is still there.

Walk around and listen to music and then go back to your place of memory. Think about the data you have stored do you remember it in your head?

Are you able to see the saved photo?

If yes do that, then you've successfully built memories palace. All you have to do now is to continuously upgrade your memory palace by adding more information and expand the range of your photography memory.

You can build multiple memory palaces in your brain that contain diverse content. Your brain is capable of handling so more than you imagine and don't think that it's too much.

Visualize your learning

While you master the new skill by rapid learning, you should imagine the whole procedure. For instance, let's say you're trying to master how to cook the best spaghetti you can find in your city.

Then you're ready to cook the recipe. You look over the recipe to attempt to picture everything from the moment you begin to prepare ingredients, until the time you cook. It is important to feed your brain with lots of colors as you cook.

Imagine the bell peppers that you'll be using as well as how long the pasta will be, color of the sauce, even the sound emanating from the kitchen. When you arrive in the kitchen and begin cooking, you'll discover that you can depend on the information you had in mind prior to.

When you're done cooking, you'll have saved all the details about the entire process into your memory. If you ever are planning to cook spaghetti you will not have to go through the recipe word-for-word no more. You'll have clear images of how you can cook your dish.

Through visualizing the process of learning by visualizing the learning process, you can increase the capacity of your photography memory, absorbing particulars and getting acquainted with all aspects.

When you're required to complete the same task in a more efficient manner then you will exceed the deadline since you're equipped with the memory of a photographer.

Photographic memory can also work well with other technical abilities when it comes to rapid learning. This is due to the fact that it lets you replicate an activity multiple times and this is why people call you"Expert. "Expert."

All you needed to do was to visualize the process inside your head. Visualization occurs by snapping pictures using your eyes and then the brain stores it. Have you ever heard classical music, or been at the opera?

If you did been there, you would be amazed at the capability that the orchestra was able to play in a way that was organized without reading on any piece of paper at all times. They were able to imagine the entire show in their minds and create photographic memories.

Therefore, when it comes to the time for shows in various cities, they can perform due to the ability to visualize. Similar principles apply to actresses and actors who are so adept at a particular job that they are awarded an Oscar.

What did the actors do to make themselves be noticed? They harnessed the power of visualization using the use of a photographic memory.

When you next want to master something, do not do it by doing it passively! Learning passively is when you go through the information or do something while not paying attention and imagining the entire process.

Keep as much information about the ability and when you next need to complete the same task you'll surely be amazed by your speed. You'll have your mind readily at hand to access the photography sources you require to work faster and faster.

With a well-developed photographic memory and other abilities, you've created, you're ready for the next chapter in our travels. The next chapter will focus on self-development!

If you are required to stop reading, then stop for a moment.

We're about to enter the final chapter and it is packed with a number of ideas that will complete the accelerated learning program you have been enrolled in.

Conclusion

You've got it, everything you need to master new information as well as skills fast and to apply those skills to great use. Your brain is an incredible organ that can keep more information than most might think I'm hoping this book has given you at the very least a tiny glimpse of the potential it has.

You will realize that there are many ways to utilize the information you have around you , information that you used to dismiss as unimportant or unimportant. You'll be successful in every aspect you do to do, and you're going discover that this really will make a difference to your life.

It can be difficult, but I am aware that the more you're willing to put in the effort as well as the longer you apply the knowledge you've acquired the easier it's going to be to master (and keep) additional techniques in your day-to- daily life.

As exercise every day strengthens your body and makes it capable of handling more and greater pressure, so does your brain functions, too. The more you are able to practice studying and remembering what you've learned the more likely you will be to discover that your brain desires to know more, and also to keep the information you read, listen to and observe.

Your brain is built to function at its maximum ability, and to make sure that it can do that you will be required to play your part. You will discover that learning speed accelerates your life and not just be wondering how you got through in the first place but you will also be wondering how the people that you see on the street live their lives on their mobile phones and internet for everything else.

You'll get a fresh perspective on the world and will be amazed at the value you gain from a simple ability. I hope that this book was an inspiration to you and that you will take the lessons you learned here to the heart. There are plenty of opportunities available, waiting for you to start to the right place.

What are you wasting time for? Now that you have mastered new abilities by reading the help of this guide, but you've also acquired the skills you need to develop more and greater skills, based on the knowledge you've acquired in the present and what you'll be able to learn in the near future. Don't stop learning, don't ever stop learning but most important of all:

www.ingramcontent.com/pod-product-compliance
Lightning Source LLC
Chambersburg PA
CBHW060333030426
42336CB00011B/1313